Developing Children'
Social, Emotional and
Behavioural Skills

C000004731

Also available from Continuum

Developing Children's Emotional Intelligence – Shahnaz Bahman and Helen Maffini

Emotional and Behavioural Difficulties – Roy Howarth and Pam Fisher

Helping Young People to Beat Stress – Sarah McNamara

Developing Children's Social, Emotional and Behavioural Skills

Márianna Csóti

continuum

Continuum International Publishing Group

The Tower Building
11 York Road
SE1 7NX

80 Maiden Lane
Suite 704
New York, NY 10038

www.continuumbooks.com

British Library Cataloguing-in-Publication Data

A catalogue record for this book is available from the British Library.

ISBN-10 (paperback): 1-8553-9471-5
ISBN-13 (paperback): 978-1-8553-9471-1

Library of Congress Cataloging-in-Publication Data

A catalog record for this book is available from the Library of Congress.

Typeset by Newgen Imaging Systems Pvt Ltd, Chennai, India
Printed and bound in Great Britain by Athenaeum Press Ltd., Gateshead, Tyne & Wear

Contents

Introduction

The importance of teaching social, emotional and behavioural skills to both primary and secondary school pupils has never been greater. The Every Child Matters: Change for Children agenda places an emphasis on the well-being of all children, aged 0–19. It aims to improve the lives of children and their families by delivering a programme that takes into account five outcomes (shown below) that have been found to matter to children most. These five outcomes have been further subdivided.

Be healthy. Children should be: physically healthy, mentally and emotionally healthy and sexually healthy. Children should have healthy lifestyles and choose not to take illegal drugs.

Stay safe. Children should stay safe from: maltreatment, neglect, violence and sexual exploitation, accidental injury and death, bullying and discrimination, crime and anti-social behaviour in and out of school. Children should also have security, stability and be cared for.

Enjoy and achieve. Children should: be ready for school, attend and enjoy school, achieve stretching national educational standards at primary school and secondary school, achieve personal and social development and enjoy recreation.

Make a positive contribution. Children should: engage in decision making and support the community and environment, engage in law-abiding and positive behaviour in and out of school, develop positive relationships and choose not to bully and discriminate, develop self-confidence and successfully deal with significant life changes and challenges, develop enterprising behaviour.

Achieve economic well-being. Children should: engage in further education, employment or training on leaving school, be ready for employment, live in decent homes and sustainable communities, have access to transport and material goods, live in households free from low income. Economic well-being can follow from a successful school career.

Another relatively recent government initiative which aims to promote the teaching of social, emotional and behavioural skills at primary and secondary level is Social and Emotional Aspects of Learning (SEAL). The programme identifies five qualities and skills that underpin children's ability to manage life, learn effectively, get on with other people and help them become responsible citizens: self-awareness, managing feelings, motivation, empathy and social skills.

SEAL aims to help children make and sustain positive relationships, manage their own emotions, thoughts and behaviour, stand up for their rights and not violate other people's rights, respect other people's values and beliefs, work cooperatively, resolve conflict, solve problems alone or with other people, be able to empathize with other people, be self-motivated, be effective and successful learners and be able to promote calm and optimistic states that promote the achievement of goals, recover from setbacks and persist in the face of difficulties.

In the past, the acquisition of these skills has very often been left up to chance but now schools have taken these initiatives on board and are incorporating them into their citizenship and personal, social and health education (PSHE) programmes as well as into general teaching.

The emphasis of this book is on learning and using social and assertiveness skills, maximizing personal potential and managing self-doubt, low self-esteem and emotions that interfere with relationships and life's progression.

As with any new skill, repetition reinforces the work already done, but children should also be encouraged to put what they learn into practice. The topics in the book can be addressed in the order they come in, or particular issues that might be especially helpful can be picked out. Some of what you choose to teach may also be age or skills dependent – for example, some topics might be too basic and you might want to skip over them quickly; others might involve too high a level of social skill.

However, even with the demand for higher levels of social awareness, the information and ideas may be adapted to suit the class you have at the time. For example, being able to empathize with other people is a high level social skill, but a young child could be encouraged to imagine it is her, rather than her friend's, pet hamster that has just died. She could imagine that her friend might appreciate a hug or hearing her say how sorry she is that he's lost his hamster and that she'd feel upset if her dog died.

Although most of the material is suitable for primary-age children much of it can still be used with secondary-age children. Some material in this book is clearly only intended for secondary use, such as the references to pregnancy, drugs and alcohol. However, these ideas are still appropriate to use with younger children, giving alternative examples to the ones provided.

A variety of approaches to delivering the content of the book have been used to appeal to many different learning styles, to deliver information in the most appropriate form and to provide variety and enjoyment to allay boredom, increasing the likelihood that children remain engaged. As well as being relevant to the children, this material should be fun to follow – it helps to have a lively and enthusiastic teacher!

Activities – which I would describe as non-passive tasks – include group or class discussions, creating lists or sentences, telling anecdotes, demonstrating how sentences should be spoken or how food should be eaten, commenting on someone else's delivery of a message, predicting when something would be appropriate or inappropriate and carrying out group exercises to illustrate a point. Role plays are used to show social pitfalls and how much more skilled the children can become, putting what they learn into practice.

You may also find this book useful when teaching children with special educational needs. Children diagnosed with an autism spectrum disorder (ASD) such as Asperger syndrome do not naturally pick up social skills as they grow up and have to be taught them in a formal way. Many children with attention deficit hyperactivity disorder (ADHD) also have difficulty following social rules – they might, for example, find it hard to wait for their turn in a game or to wait to be invited to answer a question and instead blurt it out. Other children might have poor social skills because their parents are not skilled communicators or feel awkward in social situations and so are not useful role models for their children. Some children do have socially skilled parents but for some reason have failed to observe and copy positive social behaviour.

An awareness of social skills deficits alerts you to the need for using unambiguous language when speaking to children and giving very clear body language messages. For example, teasing some children might be inappropriate as the friendliness of the gesture could well be misinterpreted as dislike and hostility. For children with ASD the choice of words needs to be carefully considered – telling a child he needs to pull his socks up might get him struggling to pull up socks that don't need pulling up while he puzzles over why you should mention them, when you really meant that he needed to try harder and apply more effort to the task in progress.

Praise is vital when children demonstrate positive social skills since their ability to display them is often dependent on their self-esteem. If they feel good about themselves they will have greater confidence in trying out what they learn – and a greater chance of becoming socially successful in their school life, their home life and leisure time and, later, in their working life.

To help children develop social, emotional and behavioural skills, all school staff members need to be seen to be using them; no child will learn respect, for example, if he or she is not treated with respect by those acting as role models. The most important person in the school to drive these skills forward is the headteacher – and the importance of children acquiring these skills needs to be written into school policy.

In running the activities described in this book it is important for all children to be clear about respecting others. In group work, children should agree on rules that they should all keep to such as:

- Don't interrupt someone already talking.

- Don't laugh at anything anyone says – unless a joke was intended.

- If you disagree, be prepared to say why.

- Be constructive with your criticism – suggest a way to improve something that was said or done.

- Value everyone's contribution.

- Allow all group members to have their say.

- Allow group members to stay silent if they don't wish to contribute.

- Avoid being judgemental.

- Don't use what group members say against them at a later date – and don't use it for gossip.

Developing Children's Social, Emotional and Behavioural Skills

Self-awareness

Who am I?

Thinking about the many aspects that contribute to their personal identity helps children to realign or strengthen any image they have of themselves and forces them to view themselves in a more complete fashion – rather than being overcritical about one particular aspect such as appearance.

Having a positive personal identity is crucial to high self-esteem – and this can be threatened when children feel that they, and their culture, are not valued. Children who value their culture and are proud of their ethnic group are less prone to racist bullying; their sense of self is stronger.

In thinking deeply about who they are, children can consider whether the picture they have of themselves represents exactly the kind of person they'd like to be. Shaping themselves into someone they would be proud to be raises self-esteem. To value others, they need to value themselves first.

Becoming more intimately acquainted with the self assists children in understanding that other people have similar hopes, dreams and concerns and this is vital for fostering empathy towards others and building rapport. Knowing themselves also helps early conversations when they can categorize superficial information they don't mind giving away and very personal information that they need to be wary of giving away before a trusting relationship is established.

Advice

When children know who they are, and understand why they are who they are, they become self-aware and can question their motives and behaviours when interacting with others, allowing them to respect differences and celebrate commonalities.

In considering the following questions, the children could create a small booklet about themselves:

- What are your favourite clothes? What do you like about them? What clothes do you dislike? Why is that?

- What animals, food, plants, books, music, films do you like and dislike?

- What things don't you like doing? Do you do them nevertheless or do you try to avoid doing them altogether?

- What things do you enjoy in school? Why? What things do you dislike?

- What things are good about your family? Why? Is there anything you don't like? Do you know why?

- What things make you feel happy, lonely, scared, amused, angry?

- Who do you most like, and most dislike, to be with? Why?

- What values and beliefs do you hold? Why? (Are you automatically adopting your parents' values and beliefs or have you thought deeply enough about issues to call them your own values and beliefs? Or are you diverging deliberately from the values and beliefs your parents have?)

- What do you like about being a girl/boy? What advantages do you think there are to being a girl/boy? And what are the disadvantages?

- Which words would you use to describe yourself physically and emotionally?

- What are your personal rules? (Don't lie, look out for others . . .)

- Are you proud of who you are, of your family and your culture? Why?

- What do you want out of life? What are your ambitions and dreams?

Application

Role models

Role models are usually people children look up to or admire. They could either admire them as a whole or by identifying particular traits they wish they had.

The first role models children have are their parents or carers. They could be either good role models or unhelpful role models or, most commonly, a mix of both. Other role models include friends, siblings, relations, religious leaders, teachers and celebrities. The more children are aware of the effect of other people's behaviour on their behaviour, and of other people's thoughts on their thoughts, the better they will be at monitoring themselves and shaping themselves into someone they can be proud of and admire. These things are essential to high self-esteem.

It is important for children to understand that they can change who they are at any time of their life. They will change as they get older – and become wiser. They will probably try to become better people and more understanding of other people, which helps them from rewarding and satisfying relationships.

Advice

Discuss the following questions with the class:

- What is a role model? Who were your first role models? What other role models do you have?

- Whom do you model yourself on the most in your family? Why?

- Are there characteristics you have recognized in other people that you don't like? Why?

- Are there any celebrities you admire? Why? Are there any you dislike or disapprove of? Why?

- Have you ever done something bad (such as shoplift) just to gain approval from someone else or to make you part of a group? How did this make you feel? Do you regret doing bad things just to please someone else?

- Have you ever forced someone to do something bad – or laughed at them for not doing it? How do you think this made them feel? How did it make you feel? (Strong and powerful or guilty and uncomfortable?)

- What kind of role model would you like to be for other people? What characteristics would you show? Are these positive or negative? Examples:

Positive characteristics	Negative characteristics
Considerate	Scary
Responsible	Rude
Caring	Hostile
Kind	Violent
Fair	Judgemental
Trustworthy	Immature
Polite	Hot tempered
Friendly	Being a liar
Honest	Being a thief
Mature	Being a bully

Application

Sharing thoughts and feelings

The way children think and feel about things tells them a great deal about who they are. When children share their thoughts and feelings, the other person can say they feel the same (which is empathizing – see page 76). Or they can say they are sorry the child feels that way (which is sympathizing). Alternatively, they can suggest a different way of looking at the situation which helps children modify their thoughts and feelings to show them a more useful way of looking at, and feeling about, the problem.

Sharing thoughts and feelings helps build rapport (see page 74) between two or more people if they have similar views and feelings. This is why children tend to mix with people with whom they have things in common; they get a warmer feeling when talking about things that the other person is interested in, or feels strongly about, and when they have had similar experiences.

Talking about concerns children have helps them to problem solve. The person they tell might have some ideas about how they can approach the problem, or suggest someone who can help. Sometimes just talking about the problem out loud helps children to visualize it more clearly, leading them to a solution of their own.

Advice

Activity 1

In small groups or pairs ask the children to talk about the following:

- What things make you feel happy? Why?
- What things have people said that make you feel happy? Why?

Understanding what makes you happy, and why, is understanding part of yourself. Consider the same questions about feeling scared, angry and frustrated.

Activity 2

In small groups or pairs ask the children to talk about the following:

- When you feel sad, what things could you do to help reduce your sadness? (Talk to a friend, a parent, a teacher, do more things that make you feel happy.)
- When friends feel sad, what could you do to help? (Ask why they feel sad and listen to what they have to say. Offer to spend breaktimes with them, share your sweets with them and suggest you meet up over the weekend. If you are worried about them, talk to your teacher or your parents about it.)

Activity 3

In small groups or pairs ask the children to talk about the following:

- Do you show others that you care? (Do you notice when someone looks sad or angry and try to find out what happened to make them feel that way? Do you make an effort to be nice when you know that someone is upset about something? Do you protect someone who is being picked on?)
- How can you show that you value another person? (By asking that person about their thoughts and feelings. Making an effort to find out how they feel about something or what they think of something shows them that they are valued – and they are more likely to feel the same about you. This creates mutual liking and respect – and builds rapport between you.)

Application

Understanding limitations

By being conscious of their weaknesses, children become more self-aware and more forgiving of other people's vulnerabilities, which helps them to get on with people better. Being self-aware shows children where they need to spend their energy and imagination to try to correct failings or to improve certain personal qualities they feel are lacking. If, for example, they are poor at making friends and can recognize this, they can watch how other people make friends and notice the kinds of things they do and say that help their friendships, or they can ask for help or advice from someone else.

If children know they find something hard, it does not necessarily mean they should not do it. Instead, they could say to themselves that they can't do it yet or that with practice they'll become better. This helps build resilience (see page 126) – the ability to cope successfully with life challenges.

Some perceived shortcomings – such as appearance – can't be changed so children need to try to accept them. Lowering expectations by not, for example, comparing themselves to supermodels or professional footballers and concentrating on other qualities can help.

Advice

Discuss the following questions with the class:

- Think about your school subjects. Is there something that you find hard? Focus on one thing and consider what you could do to make that better. (Ask a friend, teacher or parent to help you, try to listen extra hard during lessons, take time at home to read through your notes to help you follow the next lesson.) Try to follow it through.

- How could you respond in a helpful way if you know a classmate finds something hard, such as games lessons? (Encourage them, 'You're nearly there . . .' and say, 'That was better than last time' and praise them, 'Well done!' Suggest you help them practise after school.)

- Is there anything you don't like about your appearance? What could you do to feel happier about it? (Try to make superficial changes that don't involve surgery or excessive dieting, but that change the way you think about your appearance.)

- Is there such a thing as a perfect person? Is it reasonable to expect that you won't make mistakes? Or other people?

- Think how it feels when someone makes fun of you. Think how it feels when someone praises you or gives you encouragement. What type of behaviour is more likely to make you give up and feel bad about yourself? What type of behaviour is likely to make you try harder and not give up? Try to remember this with your internal dialogue (when you talk to yourself in your head) and when dealing with other people. Treat other people as you would like to be treated yourself.

Application

Raising self-esteem

Self-esteem is all about how highly children regard themselves. Many things damage their self-esteem, such as being bullied, being frequently criticized, being made to feel ashamed and not having their emotional needs recognized and fulfilled.

Messages that affect self-esteem are given by family, friends, employers and other people with whom children interact. If these are overall positive messages children are more likely to have high self-esteem. Positive messages include praise, applause, smiles, hugs, plenty of eye contact, people seeking their company, laughing at their jokes and inviting them to join them in some activity. If children get overall negative messages they are likely to have low self-esteem. Negative messages include criticism, frowning, hitting, having people walk away from them or avoiding them and not making eye contact during conversation.

Having overly high expectations of themselves dents children's self-esteem, but having expectations that are too low can also give them poor self-esteem as they might never feel proud of achievements that were so easily won.

By being aware of how things affect their self-esteem children could do more of the things that help to raise it and do less of the things that contribute to lowering it. To help motivate them to do arduous things that make them feel good, children should reward themselves regularly by doing something pleasant such as seeing a friend, buying a magazine or something nice to eat, having a long bath, playing a game or surfing the internet, going shopping or to the cinema with friends.

Advice

Guide the children through the following activities and questions:

- Write down or think about all the things that people have said or done that have made you feel good about yourself and all the things that people have said or done that have made you feel bad about yourself. Which column is longer?

- How would you describe yourself? Are these adjectives positive or negative or a mix of both? What are they overall?

- Self-esteem is to do with what you think of yourself and how you think other people see you. Do you have high or low self-esteem?

- What are the consequences of having low self-esteem? (Having less motivation, less concentration, less willingness to work, less pride in your work and play, being less caring towards other people, taking less care of yourself and being at risk of depression.)

- What do you think are the consequences of having high self-esteem? (Being more responsible for yourself and other people, being less likely to pick on others, having greater motivation and concentration, being happier overall.)

- What can you do to raise your self-esteem? (Do more of the things that give you a good feeling inside and fewer of the things that give you a bad feeling inside.) Sometimes you get a bad feeling inside even if you have done nothing wrong – it may be that the problem lies with the person giving you the negative message, such as a bully, or a parent or teacher misunderstanding the situation and treating you unjustly.

- Treating yourself also raises your self-esteem. Write down what treats you could use to reward yourself for achieving something or for coping with something that was hard to do.

Application

Improving self-confidence

Children are self-confident when they have confidence in their own judgement or ability. Those who are self-confident also tend to have high self-esteem and much self-respect. Using a technique popular in neuro-linguistic programming, children can feed their confidence in times of need to help them overcome doubts in their abilities.

Ask the children to remember a time when they felt very confident and picture the scene in bright close up with vivid colours, intensifying the sounds and smells associated with it. They should only see the scene as they saw it then – as opposed to viewing it from above like an external 'all-seeing' observer – so that they are strongly associating with themselves in that scene.

Once the scene is recalled in full and they feel as confident as they did at the time, they should create an 'anchor' by saying to themselves, 'I feel incredibly confident', and assign a discreet physical gesture while saying it – one that they can feel free to use without fear of others noticing. This could be touching their hand to their thigh, closing forefinger and thumb to form an 'O', squeezing their fingers together or bending their thumb to meet their palm.

Next, the anchor needs to be well established by regularly 'firing it' – recalling the memory in full and making their discreet gesture at the peak of the intensity of the memory while saying, 'I feel incredibly confident.'

When children need to feel confident – for performing in a play or in standing up for themselves – they can 'fire' their confidence anchor. This can change the outcome of the event to one of success rather than failure, allowing them to feel more positive about themselves and more in control of their lives and their future.

Activity 1

Guide the children through the steps to create and establish an anchor for confidence. If they don't have a personal memory, they could think of a character from a book such as Harry or Hermione in the Harry Potter series or a character from a film or electronic role-play game (such as *Final Fantasy*) and carefully select a scene that shows the character in a very confident position. For example, Harry feels very confident when his Patronus spell keeps away the Dementors (*Harry Potter and the Prisoner of Azkaban*), or when he is playing Quidditch and he's the best at catching the Golden Snitch. Hermione is very confident when she identifies the plant that binds Harry and Ron in a deadly grasp as Devil's Snare (*Harry Potter and the Philosopher's Stone*) and spins a spell to make the plant release its grip.

Encourage the children to 'fire' their anchor as often as they can over the next few days – and then try to call it up at a time when their confidence needs boosting. See if they notice the difference.

Activity 2

Ask the children to select memories for positive feelings such as happy, brave, or friendly and outgoing. They should give each memory or fictional scene the same treatment as already described, with the exception of the discreet physical gesture and phrase they choose to use. These should be specific to that feeling. For example, if they choose a memory or scene that depicts them, or a character, as brave, they should say, 'I am extremely brave', while assigning a different discreet physical gesture to the one used previously.

Children can store many positive anchors for many different positive feelings and use them for protection when they feel vulnerable and to help them reach their goals (see page 111).

Application

Promoting the self

Before promoting their positive human qualities, children need to think how they'd like others to see them. What traits do they value? And why do they value them? It is better to have positive characteristics, such as being considerate, polite and caring, rather than negative characteristics, such as being cruel and a bully (although some children might want to promote a 'tough' side to avoid getting bullied, to look 'cool' or to get in with a gang).

Children can promote themselves through conversation. For example, children wanting to be seen as kind and caring people will tell stories about themselves that show they have those characteristics. And they will avoid mentioning the time they walked past an elderly man who'd dropped his shopping and they did nothing to help, or ignored the blind man who was trying to cross a road.

Children can also promote themselves through their behaviour – by changing the way they say and do things – so that their words and actions are in keeping with the characteristics they want to have. For example, they could give praise when it is deserved – being able to praise other people in a genuine way is a valuable trait and helps children to promote themselves as positive, caring people.

Discuss the following points with the class:

- For people to like, admire and respect you, you should have more positive characteristics than negative characteristics. Recall your positive characteristics from page 11. Add other positive characteristics you'd like to have and think about how you could obtain them.

- Think about everyone's need to feel successful at something and the pleasure they experience in receiving praise. Can you think of something positive to say about the person sitting next to you? Look for positive things to say about everyone in your class over the next few weeks; see it as a challenge. Children warm to positive people.

- Look for opportunities to prove that you have particular characteristics that you'd be proud to have, and then weave them into a story.

Activity

Ask the children to sit in pairs and tell anecdotes that prove they have desirable characteristics. However, they must be careful that they don't sound as if they are boasting. They should only mention one or two good things in a conversation and never say, 'I'm kind/considerate/thoughtful/funny because . . .' Instead they could say, 'On the way home I saw a man with a white stick waiting to cross the road. When I realized he was blind I offered to take him across.'

More examples:

Helpful: 'I often shop for Mum and read a story every night to my little brother.'

Kind: 'When Tom was crying I put my arm round him to help make him feel better.'

Considerate: 'When Dad had a headache I turned my music down.'

Thoughtful: 'When Daisy was feeling sad I made her a card to cheer her up.'

Fun: 'I can always make my brother laugh.'

Sympathetic: 'I feel so sorry that he lost his winning raffle ticket.'

Application

2 Communication tools

Choosing words

To communicate well, children need to have a wide 'feelings vocabulary' and describe accurately how they are feeling or how something has affected them without resorting to offensive language or destructive physical behaviour. This helps to increase their emotional literacy – being able to recognize their feelings and those of other people, and being able to manage their feelings and the feelings that arise in their relationships.

Daily use of 'feelings' words helps to encourage children to use them too. With practice, children will become more articulate and expressive, enhancing their social experiences and increasing skilful handling of their relationships. Send a letter to the children's parents explaining the work done in school and ask them to encourage the use of 'feelings' words at home.

When expressing feelings, saying, 'I don't feel well' is not as helpful as saying, 'I feel sick and my head hurts.' Saying, 'I don't want to go to the cinema' is not as helpful as saying, 'I don't feel comfortable among the crowds; they scare me.' Saying, 'I don't like her' is not as helpful as saying, 'I feel embarrassed when I'm with her because she laughed at me when I tripped up. I feel clumsy now whenever she's around.'

Advice

Having good social skills is all about being able to use effectively the tools of communication – the words children choose, how they say them and whether their facial expressions and body posture support their intended meaning.

Discuss the difference between physical feelings (how children's bodies feel) and emotional feelings (how their minds feel – although with strong emotions children also can feel them physically). Ask for examples of each and group them into positive and negative feelings? For example:

Positive emotional feelings: excited, happy, eager, proud, calm, elated.

Negative emotional feelings: anxious, frightened, sad, lonely, shy, angry, concerned, disappointed, disgusted, flustered, impatient, embarrassed.

Positive physical feelings: comfortable, alert, energetic, strong.

Negative physical feelings: cold, hot, shivery, dizzy, sick, tired, tense, weak.

Activity 1

Ask the children to make up sentences for at least two 'feelings' words from each group mentioned above. Explain that using 'feelings' words helps other people to understand them better and gets them the help and support they need if the feeling is a negative one. Discuss how, generally, negative feelings make children feel bad and positive feelings make them feel good, but that at times it's positive to feel angry or sad – these are normal reactions to life events and help children come to terms with what has happened or strengthen them in some way.

Activity 2

Ask the children to think of situations when a negative emotional feeling can be positive. Ask them to make up sentences to show how having those particular feelings is helpful.

Activity 3

Ask the children to keep a 'feelings' diary. They should collect 'feelings' words from experiencing that feeling themselves or by reading about or seeing someone experiencing that feeling.

Application

How words are spoken

Emphasizing different words in a sentence gives slightly different messages. Consider: 'You'll feed the cat now.' Stressing *you'll* suggests it's a particular person and no one else; stressing *feed* suggests the cat is to be fed and not groomed or played with; emphasizing *cat* suggests it's the cat and not another animal that is to be fed; weighting *now* indicates the immediacy of the command. By putting a question mark at the end of the sentence the command becomes a question.

The speed of speech, when it is rushed, can tell listeners that the speaker is in a hurry, or excited or angry. And when it is slow it can tell listeners whether the speaker is lazy, relaxed, sleepy or even unsure of their ground.

Pauses in speech give weight to what was just said, allow thinking time, encourage the other person to have a turn at speaking and introduce suspense in the middle of an exciting story.

The volume of speech is varied depending on where the speaker is (a church or school playground), the circumstances of the meeting (a celebration or a funeral) and how the speaker is feeling (loud for feeling angry or happy, soft for feeling sad or shy – some shy people get quieter towards the end of their sentences and some talk very quietly all the way through).

The firmness of tone can show confidence but if the voice is unsteady or wavers it can indicate nervousness or uncertainty.

Speaking in a monotone – using no variations in pitch – reduces meaning and won't keep a listener's attention. Reading a story in a monotone will fail to arouse interest in the topic or characters and will make it hard to discern which character is speaking.

Activity 1

Write 'You'll feed the cat now' on the board. Ask the children to suggest different meanings the sentence can give. Explain the importance of word emphasis in speech.

Activity 2

Read some text in a monotone. Ask the children to comment on how it sounds and invite a child to demonstrate how it should be read. Discuss the difference.

Activity 3

Write the following sentences on the board. Explain the message each is to convey and invite the children to demonstrate how they should be spoken.

- 'Oh, is that the time?' The person is in a hurry and sounds worried about being late. (Spoken quickly and breathlessly.)

- 'Don't worry. It'll be OK.' The person doesn't really care about the outcome of the listener's problem and is not taking it seriously. (Spoken slowly and dismissively.)

- 'That's just *typical* of you!' The person is angry with the listener. (Spoken loudly and sharply.)

Ask the children how they would show particular emotions through the way they say words, such as sad (speak slowly and mournfully); bored (stretch each word into a whine); excited (fast and high pitched).

Activity 4

Ask the children under what circumstances might they:

- whisper (In a place of worship, when someone is very ill or has just died, when they don't want someone to overhear, and when they don't want to disturb someone sleeping.)

- sigh (When they are disappointed, fed up, or just need to take a deeper breath than normal.)

- shout (When they are scared or need help, need someone's attention or when they are angry.).

When might it be *inappropriate* to do these things? (For example, it is considered rude to whisper in company and sigh when being told off. It is disrespectful to shout in a church.)

Application

19

Facial expressions

A face is the most expressive part of a body and can display, in addition to clearly identifiable emotions such as happiness, sadness and anger, more subtle emotions such as doubt, nervousness, hopefulness, glee and embarrassment. To demonstrate the wide variety of facial expressions there is no one better than Rowan Atkinson acting as Mr Bean. He tells very long stories almost solely through facial expression; he speaks very little yet viewers can understand everything just through watching his body language.

Some facial expressions have more than one meaning. In these situations the observer needs to understand what has gone on before to give the expression the correct interpretation. This can be hard to guess, especially for children with autism spectrum disorders. For example, a frown could indicate someone deep in thought, trying to work out a solution to a problem or trying to decide what to do – or it could indicate annoyance. Teachers frown at children who are troublesome. Children might frown when they don't understand the task set for them.

Raised eyebrows can indicate surprise, disbelief, shock or even disapproval. People squint when there is bright light or when they have poor sight and are trying to focus their eyes – but a squint can also be a threatening gesture.

Display a poster in the class depicting a range of facial expressions and encourage the children to copy some of the expressions and use them at appropriate times. Children who have difficulty expressing how they feel can point to the face that shows how they are feeling. This can be particularly useful for some children with special educational needs.

Advice

Activity 1

Show a recording of Mr Bean to the class. Ask the children to take note of how skilfully Rowan Atkinson manages to convey his intentions and his feelings mainly through facial expressions, and with a little help from the rest of his body language.

Activity 2

Ask the children to portray facially a variety of emotions, such as fear, anger, sadness, happiness, jealousy and pleasure. They should allow plenty of time to practise each expression before moving on to the next one. They could check their expressions in mirrors.

Ask the children to practise giving the right facial messages to go with a particular feeling in front of a mirror at home and try to be more expressive when they talk about their feelings with other people.

Activity 3

Devise a game whereby a volunteer is secretly given an emotion to portray non-verbally, using only facial muscles. The other children have to guess what it is. If the children need more help write a variety of sentences on the board and ask the class to guess which sentence describes what has happened to the volunteer. Suggestions include:

- You have just been given the present you always wanted. (Delight: eyes wide, mouth open and smiling in a relaxed way.)

- You have just seen a big spider. (Fear: eyes staring, mouth gaping, lips down-turned, facial muscles tense.)

- You have just been told your hamster has died. (Sadness: eyes mournful, eyelids blinking slowly and staying shut for longer than normal, down-turned mouth, facial muscles drooping.)

- You have just seen the boy/girl you fancy approaching you. (Embarrassment/shyness: repeated looking towards the floor, biting the lips, head to one side as though to hide the face.)

Application

Body language

Three qualities revealed through body posture and body gestures are passivity, aggressiveness and assertiveness.

Passivity, or timidity, is shown by mumbling or stuttering, slouching, looking down at the floor, nervously picking at fingers or biting nails, having arms folded in a protective manner with the body hunched, having legs close together to minimize space the body takes up and standing further from another person than a confident person would stand. Children who predominantly display passive body language are more open to victimization.

Aggressiveness is shown by shouting, using a sarcastic or accusing tone, having a tense upright posture where the person uses height to intimidate, staring unremittingly at the other person, having tight fists, pointing, folding arms or having hands on hips with legs more than slightly apart, standing too close to another person and invading their comfortable body space, and leaning forward in a threatening manner. Children who predominantly display aggressive body language can intimidate and find that other people are less likely to want to make friends and will probably try to avoid them.

Assertiveness is shown by speaking clearly and firmly with a well-modulated tone (not in a monotone), having a relaxed upright posture, having a gaze that meets the other person's gaze while occasionally looking away, having hands relaxed by the sides and legs slightly apart, leaning forward to talk to another person to show interest in what is being said and standing a comfortable distance from the other person. Children who show assertive body language are more likely to command respect from other people, their opinions are more likely to be valued and they are less likely to be bullied or be suspected of being bullies.

Discuss the following questions with the class:

- Passive, aggressive and assertive are words to describe certain types of behaviour. What do you know about each type of behaviour? How might passive people appear? How might aggressive people appear? How might assertive people appear?

- If someone acts confidently, people will believe that they are confident whether or not this is the case. And when people change in the way they behave towards them because they believe they are confident, that will make that person feel more confident. On the whole, how would you like to be seen? Discuss the consequences of being seen as passive, aggressive and assertive. (Also see page 97.)

Activity

Invite children to show what posture is best to adopt in the following situations:

- You are in trouble from a teacher and it is deserved. (A slightly timid posture is best to show meekness and regret. An aggressive, defiant posture is likely to get you into more trouble. A confident posture in this situation might be misinterpreted by the teacher as arrogance.)

- You are out shopping in a big town. (You need to look confident so that no one is tempted to pick on you or to try to talk you into doing something you don't want to do.)

- Someone has unjustly accused you of doing something. (You need to look outraged and angry to show you have been wronged.)

Ask the children to practise reading body language by watching people carefully when they speak – and by watching actors in films and on the television. They should also try matching their body language with the message they want to give.

Eye contact

Eye contact is used to:

- indicate which person you are talking to

- give emphasis to what you say so that you are taken seriously

- show you mean it when you say no

- show you will be able to see if the other person isn't listening

- show you have seen what the other person has done – or is about to do – which can modify their behaviour

- show you are trustworthy – you are more likely to be believed if you deny stealing something while maintaining eye contact. Dropping the gaze suggests guilt

- show dislike – by not making eye contact and effectively ignoring the other person

- show you don't like the look of someone – you tend to look away more frequently if there is something about the other person you dislike

- show you are strongly attracted to a person – you are more likely to maintain eye contact with fewer and shorter breaks and the pupils of your eyes dilate.

Unrelieved staring is aggressive or indicates a child has poor social skills. Rarely meeting someone's gaze is typical of passivity or of a timid, nervous child. It can also appear shifty, as though the child has something to hide. Usually when children are face to face their gaze does break every so often for a second or two. If a child is thinking hard or recalling something then it can break for much longer.

A lack of eye contact generally can indicate that a child is depressed – if someone in your class rarely or never makes eye contact consider this as a possibility. It may be that the child needs help.

Discuss the importance of making eye contact, the different purposes it serves and the different messages it can give. Ask the children to describe some situations when eye contact is essential. Suggestions:

- When the teacher wants to say something very important and needs to see that everyone is paying attention.

- When they want to ask someone a question – they call that person's name and look at their eyes to see when they have their attention.

- When they first greet someone. They need to say hello while looking into the other person's eyes.

- When assuring someone that they are telling the truth.

Activity

Explain that as well as showing someone they are listening, their eyes can give away their emotions. If children dislike someone – or even hate them – it shows in their eyes.

Ask the children to use only their eyes and the muscles around their eyes to show emotions of hate, anger, sadness and love. Just tiny movements in the muscles around the eyes can tell a great deal about the way a person is feeling. If the children allow the rest of their facial muscles to express the emotion it can be seen very clearly.

Application

Using communication tools

Although the different elements of communication have been looked at in some detail, children might find it hard to put these things together. Taking part in role plays can help them consolidate this work.

In each scenario described on the next page ask the children to think about how they would feel in that situation and choose words that would show this. They also need to consider how they would say those words, how their faces would look, whether they would make eye contact and what their body might be doing to back up what they say and how they feel.

Some people are very skilled at deliberately giving false messages through their body language to con people or to get someone else into trouble. Some people are specially trained to read tiny changes in the way someone looks or moves to glean more from the person than they are conscious of giving away. Psychologists use this skill to try to find out what their client is really thinking or feeling, leading them to a better understanding of the person which allows them to be more helpful in therapy. Police use this skill to try to expose people who are lying. Revealing body language for lying includes blushing, sweating, a lack of eye contact, a tense posture, chewing the lip, and scratching the nose or rubbing the jaw.

Advice

Activity 1

Ask for two volunteers, A and B. Give them a slip of paper that provides a script for a scenario that they act out. The rest of the class must guess how B is feeling. How do they know? Could B improve his/her body language to give a clearer message? The scenario can be repeated using all the suggestions the class has made. Have new volunteers for each script.

Suggestions include:

- A: 'Here's a present for you.'
  B: 'This is just what I wanted.' You feel *delighted*.

- A: 'I'm sorry, I can't come to your party after all.'
  B: 'Oh no. What a shame.' You feel *disappointed*.

- A: 'I saw you take money from my bag!'
  B: 'Oh. Sorry.' You feel *ashamed*.

- A: 'This is what I think of your new CD-ROM game.' (Mime snapping it in two.)
  B: 'Why did you do that?' You feel extremely *angry*.

- A: 'I just heard your best friend had an accident and has had to go to hospital.'
  B: 'Oh no.' You feel very *concerned*.

- A: 'The caretaker's cat's died.'
  B: 'Oh, poor caretaker. Poor cat.' You feel very *sad*.

- A: 'Hey, I won that competition.'
  B: 'That's wonderful!' You feel very *pleased*.

- A: 'Would you like to come with my family on Saturday to that theme park we talked about?'
  B: 'Would I? Yes please!' You feel very *excited*.

- A: 'It's your exam this morning isn't it?'
  B: 'Yeeeesss.' You feel *scared*.

- A: 'I don't want to be friends with you any more.
  B: 'Oh. Why not?' You feel *hurt*.

Activity 2

Ask volunteers to make prepared statements to the class. Are they telling the truth? How do the children know?

3

Social rules and roles

Classroom social rules

Each class has its own social rules such as:

- When the teacher asks for the class's attention the children should stop what they are doing, stop talking and look at the teacher.

- If children wish to answer a question, they must put up their hands and wait to be invited to answer. No one should call out answers or make fun of someone else's answer.

- When working as a team, children must share out the tasks and apparatus/materials fairly. They should listen to the ideas the others in the team have and consider them. If they reject the ideas, they should be able to explain to the person why.

- When handing out books or equipment the items should be placed gently on the tables, not thrown.

- There must be no pushing, shoving or snatching. No shouting or screaming.

- When a child speaks to someone he/she should look that person in the eye.

- If children are late, they must apologize to the teacher and give an explanation.

- If, when a child comes in, the door is shut, it must be closed again afterwards.

Advice

Children are expected to know how to behave in all kinds of situations, yet are rarely formally taught social rules. By not observing such rules they can find themselves in trouble and without friends.

Discuss the school rules and why schools have them. (To keep order, to make things fair so that everyone is treated the same, to enable the school to run efficiently and safely, to help children live as responsible adults later in life, to show that all groups in society have rules to abide by which help people get along with one another.)

Activity 1

Ask the children to make up a list of class rules – if they haven't already been given a list. Why are these rules needed? (They help teach respect, help children to take turns and be considerate towards others, and help to create an environment that is favourable to learning and cooperation.)

Activity 2

Children will be encouraged to stick to the rules if they see that there are rules for teachers too. This helps to foster mutual respect and emphasizes the position of the teacher as an effective role model. Ask the children to make up rules for teachers. Below are some suggestions.

Teachers should:

- apologize if late and explain why
- mark homework promptly and apologize if it is handed back late
- treat the class with respect and not poke fun at or humiliate pupils
- teach the lesson with enthusiasm and try to make it interesting
- use a variety of methods to control the class and not just shout
- try to share their time equally between the children in the class
- value the class members as individuals and understand their strengths and weaknesses.

Application

Running an errand in school

When running an errand, children must understand what's required of them to fulfil the need of the person making the request. But also they must understand school etiquette. For example, a teacher gives a girl a note to pass to another teacher. She must accept the note proffered – not snatch it out of the teacher's hand. When she leaves the classroom she should shut the door quietly behind her (assuming it has not been purposely left ajar) – rather than slam it – and walk sedately down the corridor – rather than run, skip or hop – until reaching the door to the classroom of the other teacher. There she should pause and give a measured knock rather than rush straight up to the door and bang hard. She should listen for a teacher to say 'come in' but if she hasn't heard anything and feels the knock would have been heard, she may slowly open the door and enter.

On entering, the child's gaze should seek the teacher – not roam the class for friends to pull faces at – and she should not go over to a table of children and start a conversation. Once she has spotted the teacher, she should go over and, standing in a position that catches the teacher's gaze, wait to be invited to speak – the teacher might be in the middle of explaining something to another child. After explaining that she has brought a note, the child should wait to see if there is to be a message back. She should then quietly leave and return promptly to her own class – without meandering down the corridor admiring artwork or using the opportunity to eat sweets.

Role play

Ask for three volunteers: two 'teachers' and a child to run an errand.
Divide the class into two, where one side has the teacher who wants to
send a child on an errand and that child – plus some classmates – and
the other side has the 'class' where the teacher is to receive the message.
The division between the two 'classes' can represent the corridor outside
the classrooms.

Explain to the three children what their roles are and privately explain to
the child running the errand how he/she is to perform the task – as badly
as possible. To help the observers understand what behaviour is being
mimed, the child could talk aloud, 'Oh, that's a nice picture, who painted
that? What's this? A concert for parents . . .?'

Ask the children in the two 'classes' to think about the expected behaviour
of a child running an errand. Then ask them to watch what the child
running the errand does and, without calling out, mentally note the
mistakes he/she makes.

After the role play, invite the children to suggest a mistake they spotted.
How many others found the same one? Discuss it. If they identified
a mistake in error, discuss that. Discover which child found the most
mistakes. Ask for a volunteer to demonstrate how an errand should be
done.

Another scenario that could be role-played: A child has been sick in class.
A volunteer is needed to tell the school secretary (to ring the child's
parents), and the caretaker (to help clean up the mess).

Invent errands for the children to do so that they can practise what they
have learned.

Table manners

Essential rules for polite eating:

Do

- go to the loo beforehand so that you won't interrupt the meal
- wash your hands
- use cutlery unless other people are using their fingers
- pick up food which you have dropped on the floor and put it on the edge of your plate, on the table or in the bin – don't eat it.

Don't

- grab food for your plate – use serving utensils if provided, but don't use them to eat with
- pile food too high on your plate in case there isn't enough to go round and in case you can't eat it
- eat with your mouth open
- steal food from other people's plates or eat directly from a serving dish
- use your own cutlery to take food from a serving dish
- put food back on a serving plate once you've fingered it or if it has been on your plate
- eat or drink noisily
- whisper at the table – other people will think you are talking about them
- talk with your mouth full or talk about toilet or vomiting issues
- break wind or belch.

Environment-dependent rules

In school you can eat with your elbows on the table and talk while eating. At a friend's house, you should wait for permission before you start eating – and before you leave the table. Wait to be invited to have second helpings, and thank the person who cooked the meal.

At a restaurant, open the napkin and place it on your lap; use it to wipe your mouth or fingers but never for blowing your nose. Start to eat when everyone's meal arrives, and at the end of the meal thank the person paying. Don't leave the table until everyone is ready to go.

Advice

Discuss table manners to produce a list of dos and don'ts.

Discuss the differences in expectations when children eat in school, at a friend's house and in a restaurant, and when eating with different people. (These might be dependent on culture or status or vary according to how well they know the person.)

Activity

Give the children clean sets of plastic cutlery and plates. Ask them to position a knife, fork, soup spoon and dessertspoon around their plate. (Dessertspoons go above the plate with the handle pointing towards their right hand – assuming right-handedness. Soup spoons rest to the right of the knife.) Then ask these questions:

- How would you eat soup? (Don't slurp, tilt the bowl and spoon away from you.)

- Can you use the knife and fork together to cut imaginary food?

- Show how you would transport solid food to your mouth. (It is rude to bow your head low over the plate; the cutlery – fork or spoon – should be brought up to your mouth with your head still. The knife is never used to bring food to your mouth and should never be put in your mouth.)

- Where should your knife and fork go when you have finished your meal? (They should be placed neatly together on the plate – at the six o'clock position or slightly to either side of this.)

Discuss cultural differences. (Usually, Muslims and Hindus eat with their right hand – their left hand is 'unclean'. Belching while at the table is considered complimentary by people in Korea and in other parts of South East Asia. In some parts of South East Asia, Israel and North Africa it is rude to empty your plate completely as it suggests you have not had enough to eat.)

General social rules

Children gain ideas about polite or expected social behaviour from their parents and other adult family members, from their time in school, from books, from the television and from watching other children with their families. Many children fall foul of socially acceptable behaviour because they haven't heard rules openly spoken about or they aren't given an explanation of what they have done wrong when told off. It is important not to assume that all children have the same social experience with families prioritizing polite behaviour or even being aware of social conventions.

Many social rules are cultural. For example, in Russia, you must not shake hands or kiss over the threshold of a doorway as it is considered bad luck. In some Arab countries and in much of South East Asia, it is rude to show the soles of your feet. Blowing your nose in public in Arab countries and South East Asia is considered rude, especially if done at the table. In South East Asia you should not use cloth handkerchiefs but disposable tissues – and once a tissue has been used it must be thrown away, not saved for later use.

Discuss the importance of social rules and what they are for.

Activity

Make up a list of social dos and don'ts. (Many rules can be relaxed when with close family members or friends.)

Do	Don't
Say please and thank you at appropriate times, such as when you want someone to pass you something.	Go to the loo in public.
Kiss family members at appropriate times, such as at bedtime and when greeting or saying goodbye.	Touch or play with your genitals or breasts (for adolescent girls) in public.
Say hello and smile when meeting someone (this is not something a child should do with a stranger if they have not been introduced).	Pick your nose or burp or break wind in public.
Sound and look pleased to see the person you are greeting. Be prepared to shake hands.	Swear or be disrespectful.
Face people when you speak to them, or when they speak to you, and look them in the eye.	Laugh when someone talks about a sad or serious event.
Look pleased when you receive a gift, even if you are disappointed with it, and say thank you.	Lie or cheat.
Use people's names when you address them.	Be insincere to curry favour.
Smell and look clean unless you are involved in a mucky task.	Deliberately embarrass other people – be tactful.

Discuss cultural differences in social rules.

Family rules

It is important for children to have clear family rules so that they have clear guidelines and boundaries – otherwise they can get into trouble without understanding why. It's also helpful to know which rules are more serious to break. These might be rules to do with keeping them and other family members safe and being polite and respectful.

Send a letter home asking parents to support the work done in school by making up a list of rules for their family with the help of their child/children. Once done, the list can be displayed in a prominent place such as on the freezer or on a kitchen cupboard to remind all family members about the rules. Having family rules that all members have contributed to clarifies the expected behaviour for that family and should help it run more smoothly. Children tend to feel more secure when they have clear guidelines on which to act. However, consistency is needed within a family to make this work. For example, the same penalty should happen every time a rule is broken. Perhaps also, families might like to start a reward system for positive actions by family members.

Advice

Discuss why it is helpful to have clear family rules.

Activity

Ask the children to form groups to make up a list of family rules.
These might be rules that they feel families should have even if their family
doesn't have them. Suggestions include:

Do	Don't
Be obedient.	Hurt or threaten another family member.
Be respectful and polite.	Steal or borrow something without permission.
Wash your hands before eating.	Forget to say sorry if you have done something wrong.
Eat without fuss.	Eat with elbows on the table, chew food with an open mouth or talk with your mouth full.
Ask to be excused if you want to leave the table before everyone else.	Search through other family members' possessions.
Be safe – ask permission to use kitchen equipment or the iron or sharp instruments.	Invade other family members' privacy when changing, going to the loo or showering/bathing.
Show appreciation of what other family members do.	Make noise late at night or early in the morning.
Help with household chores. Keep your own space in the home clean and tidy as well as yourself.	Repeat your parents' conversations outside the home.
Wipe your feet when you enter your home and remove outdoor shoes.	Deliberately embarrass other family members.
Get on with your homework.	Answer back or call family members rude names.

Ask children to discuss family rules at home and produce a clear set of rules
to help the way in which their family runs.

Rules outside school

There are rules in every environment, including shops, cinemas, places of worship, swimming pools, gyms, sports fields, trains, buses and planes. Sometimes rules that involve the law are made clear – for example, shops display signs that shoplifters will be prosecuted. We need rules to help keep order and to keep people safe. When people fail to behave socially in the expected way they are called anti-social.

Expected behaviour in cinemas includes queuing quietly for tickets, paying for entry, switching off mobile phones, sitting quietly and without fidgeting during the showing, eating and drinking quietly and trying to prevent spillages of food and drink. It would be anti-social to do any of these or to stick chewing gum onto the seats or onto the backs of other viewers.

Expected behaviour at a swimming pool includes queuing quietly and paying for entry, changing into suitable clothing, showering before entering the pool, not jumping into the pool where other people might get hurt, making sure other swimmers don't get splashed, not diving into the shallow end, paying attention to the lifeguard, not running along the edge of the pool, not bumping into babies or young children who are just learning to be confident in the pool, not trying to drown someone (even as a joke), not drinking or eating in the pool area, not going to the loo in the pool and not kissing or fondling someone in the pool. Some of these rules are to do with safety and others are related to being considerate towards people.

Advice

Discuss the rules found in society outside school. Explain the need for them.

Discuss the following questions with the class:

- What is anti-social behaviour? Give examples. (Suggestions: singing loudly or playing loud music in public, shoplifting, deliberately spoiling goods on sale, creating graffiti, smashing windows, breaking telephones and pulling out cables, sticking chewing gum on school furniture, pretending you are under-age for train, bus or cinema tickets, dodging fares or sneaking into the cinema without paying, talking throughout a film or public performance, eating noisily in the cinema and harassing customers, making fun of complete strangers, becoming drunk in public, going to the loo in public or making a mess in a public loo, spitting, bullying, intimidating people.)

- Why are some children deliberately anti-social? (They do it to show off, to be thought of as cool or to seek approval from gang members.)

- Have any of you experienced anti-social behaviour? What happened and how did you feel about it?

- Have you ever been anti-social? Why? What did you do? What were people's reactions to your behaviour? How do you feel about it now?

- What makes a good neighbour? (Suggestions: keeping a spare key in case you get locked out, looking after your home while you're away on holiday, letting a plumber in to do some emergency work, making sure they don't make too much noise especially late at night or early in the morning at weekends – and in the daytime if someone works night shifts – being friendly and being keen to help when you are in trouble.) Why is it important to have a good neighbour? (Each of you can be considerate to the other – it helps to build a caring community.)

Application

Roles

Expected behaviour is determined by the role that the person is playing at the time – and the role of the person with whom they interact. Sometimes these people are equal as in friend/friend or pupil/pupil. Then the expectations of behaviour for each of the pair would be the same. However, unequal pairs, such as pupil/teacher, daughter/mother, son/father, customer/shopkeeper, patient/doctor, require different behaviour for each person.

Sometimes the place that the pair is in determines the expected behaviour. For example, when two friends are outdoors, playing in the street or park, their expected behaviour is identical. But when a child is taken home by a friend that friend has the additional requirement of being host to a guest.

Advice

Discuss the following questions with the class:

- The behaviour someone expects from you depends on the role you are playing at the time. What roles do you have?

- What behaviour is expected with these roles?

Son/daughter	Be polite, respectful, obedient, loving and appreciative of the things done for you. Help with household chores.
Sibling	Help care for them. Keep them safe. Amuse them. Help with homework. Give advice. Be a friend.
Friend	Be fun to be with. Laugh at their jokes. Keep them company. Share the same kinds of interests. Enjoy doing things together. Show care.
Pupil	Be punctual. Have the right books, writing equipment, PE kit and packed lunch or dinner money. Listen while the teacher talks. Do your work quietly and without complaint. Do your homework. Be respectful to the teacher and do as you're told.
Neighbour	Try not to let balls go over the fence if you live next door to someone with a garden. If a ball does go over, knock on the door to ask permission to get it. Try to keep the noise down. Never ring the doorbell and run off. Be polite and friendly. If the neighbour is old or sick, offer to get shopping for them or walk their dog.
Guest	Be appreciative of any food or drink you are given and be polite. Be prepared to have fun and be good company. Be careful of breaking or spoiling anything. Say, 'Thank you for having me round' when you leave.
Host	Offer a drink or something to eat. Help your friend have fun. Show them where the loo is if necessary. Be careful about spillages and breakages from careless behaviour – don't show off!
Employee	Be punctual, polite and respectful. Work hard.

4

Interacting with other people

Meeting and greeting

Meeting someone often involves a measure of 'oiling the wheels' to develop the relationship. When children meet someone they know, they are meant to look pleased to see them by smiling and making eye contact, and the other person must sound pleased to see them. 'Hello' should not be said in a monotone – which indicates a lack of interest – but in a lively and warm way. Looking away suggests they wish they hadn't seen the person or hope he or she will soon go away. This can make him/her feel hurt and rejected.

However, not looking pleased to see someone might have nothing to do with how children feel about them – they might be running late and might not have time to talk. If this is so, children should explain why they must hurry away to prevent bruising the other person's feelings. The next time they meet they should make an extra effort to talk. If they don't that person will definitely feel that they are unimportant to them and this will start to make them unpopular. Children like people who show they like them.

There are many occasions when children need to interact with other people. Even simple tasks such as meeting someone or answering the telephone involve complex social behaviour.

Role play 1

Ask two volunteers, A and B, to greet each other. Invite the class to comment on whether they seemed pleased to see each other. Could the greeting be done in a more positive manner? Repeat the role play with improvements. Suggestion:

A: (Smiles) 'Hello B.' (Stops walking and faces B.)

B: (Smiles) 'Hi. How are you?/What's news?/What are you doing here?'

Role play 2

Ask three volunteers, A, B and C, to act out a scene where A and B are friends chatting. C approaches. C is friends with A but does not know B. What should A do? (A should not ignore C's approach or ignore B after C has arrived. She should introduce C to B and B to C and then try to include C in their conversation.) Suggestion:

A: (Smiles) 'Hi C. This is B, a friend from my road. (Turns to face B.) This is C – she goes to school with me.'

C and B: (Smile) 'Hi.'

A: 'We were just talking about . . .'

Role play 3

Ask for two volunteers, A and B. A knocks at the door of a friend's house. B, the friend's mother, opens the door. A greets B. Suggestion:

A: (Smiles widely.) 'Hello Mrs X, is Martha in? Could I see her?'

B: 'Hello A. Yes she is. Come in.'

If the opportunity arises, A could make a positive comment such as, 'Have you painted the hallway? It looks very smart/a lovely colour.'

Application

Saying goodbye

It is sometimes hard to say goodbye without causing offence, especially when another person is talking. You can't interrupt mid-sentence to mutter goodbye and then walk off: it would make the other person feel as if they'd been boring you, which could embarrass them. They could also feel angry that you ignored what they were saying; it might make them dislike you.

Ideally, a child in this situation should start to show body language cues that they are ready, or need, to go, such as picking up shopping or a school bag, or adjusting the bag on their shoulder or even changing it to the other shoulder. They could handle keys and increase breaks in eye contact, slightly turning their body away and taking a small step in the direction they need to go.

If the other person is skilled, they will have noticed by now that the child needs to go and will quickly finish their story and either allow a pause for the child to say they need to go or would ask if the child needs to go – and they'll both say their goodbyes around the same time because they are both ready for the performance of leave-taking. However, if the speaker takes no notice of the child's cues, that child could look at a watch and gasp, 'Oh. I must go! I'm going to be late. I promised my sister I'd meet her . . .' Or they could mention the train they've got to catch. If they add that they'll see the person again soon – or that it was nice having the chat – it softens the leave-taking. It can be further softened by touching the other person's arm as they leave.

Role play

Ask for two volunteers, A (who must be talkative) and B (who needs to be shy). A and B are on their way home from school and are chatting at a street corner with their bags on the floor. A chats without pause. B must find a way to leave – she's got one minute to do it in or she misses her train home!

Invite the class to comment on how this was achieved. Did B give A plenty of cues showing she needed to leave? Or did she just interrupt rudely or walk off without saying anything? How could the role play be improved? Ask the volunteers to repeat the role play. Suggestion:

A: Chats constantly.

B: Picks up her bag, changes the hand it's held in, puts it on one shoulder then shifts it to the next. Gets her train pass (or money) out of her pocket and fingers it. Her gaze flits more and more away from B's face. She turns her body slightly away and has her feet face the direction she needs to go in. She takes a step back.

A: 'Oh, do you need to go?'

B: 'Yes. Sorry, I must dash or I'll miss my train. Bye.'

A: 'Bye.'

Discuss what children should do when they are leaving a friend's house. (Say goodbye to their friends and to the adults of the household and thank them politely for having them round if they are very young. If they are older they could show gratitude by saying something like, 'It was nice to see you again. Thanks for the drink/meal.' If the adults are in a different room, they should say to their friend, 'I'd like to say goodbye to your parents.')

Shyness

Shyness is a reluctance to interact with other people through inhibition – feeling uncomfortable about performing in front of other people and feeling concerned about how other people will rate your performance. Shy behaviour can give other people the message that you don't like them and that you can't be bothered to talk, or be polite, to them which puts you at risk of becoming lonely.

Shy children can feel so awkward that they can't show interest in another person; they might believe they are uninteresting and have nothing of note to say and they might not be prepared to make the required effort of being friendly by keeping a conversation going. Both children involved in a conversation need to contribute and if one doesn't the relationship might flounder or not develop at all.

Behaviour to help reduce children's shyness includes smiling and saying hello to other children, asking a teacher a question at the end of a lesson with a friend or in the middle of a lesson on their own, offering to answer questions by raising a hand in class, volunteering to run errands, talking to children they don't normally talk to, smiling and saying hello to shop assistants who serve them, asking shop assistants for help in finding something, accepting all social invitations and joining clubs.

Shy children need to ensure that when they interact with other people they make eye contact and they speak loudly enough to be heard. They mustn't rush their speech or fail to fully explain what they are asking because of embarrassment, wanting to get the question over with. They should try to talk smoothly without jerks in the speech or stuttering or many 'ums' and 'ers' and uncomfortable silences.

Discuss the following questions with the class:

- What is shyness? How does it feel? Are you shy all the time or just some of the time? What kinds of situations make you feel shy? (New situations, when you are with people you don't know at all or not very well, when you meet up with friends after a long break, when you talk to adults, when you have to address the whole class or perform in assembly.)

- Are there any times when you don't feel shy? (When you are with friends, family or when you are on your own.)

- What do you gain from being shy? (Shyness can be an excuse not to bother to make an effort. It can also mean you get out of being asked to do things as you don't look confident enough; and you can blend in to the background and not be noticed.)

- If you weren't shy at all, what would you gain? (Having more friends, enjoying their company more, getting to know them better, having friends get to know you better, learning about the world and other people – giving you great practice for when you are older and in less familiar situations.)

- What do people look like when they are being shy? (Head bowed, eyes lowered, fingers fiddling with clothes or biting nails, shifting their feet, blushing.)

- How can you overcome shyness? (Aim for confident body language – it will help you feel more confident. Practise talking to people – if you don't know what to say, ask them about themselves and they will enjoy talking and will like you for asking.) (See Chapter 5 for further help with shyness.)

Application

Making a telephone call

Using the telephone is an important social skill, especially now that so many children have their own mobile phones, so it is important that they develop an acceptable telephone manner.

For example, a girl wants to ring a friend to ask her to come out with her for the day. Before she makes the call she needs to think carefully about what she wants to say – the reason for the call, the details of the day such as the time to arrive and the time to go home and any proposed activities, like swimming. Jotting the information down helps to remind her of what she needs to say.

Then she needs to look up her friend's telephone number and punch the numbers in very carefully. If the phone is answered by her friend's parents, or a sibling, she could say, 'Hello, it's X. Could I speak to Y please?' *'I'll just get her for you.'* 'Thank you.' If she is known to the family it is polite to declare who she is. Parents often like to know who is calling their child.

If she is a very young child and Y's parents answer, she could ask them directly whether they will let her friend come out with her, 'Hello. Is that Mr Reed? It's X. I'm calling to ask if Y can come round for the day and come swimming.'

If it is her friend who answers, the child can explain directly to her, 'Hi, it's X. I'm ringing to ask if you'd like to . . .'

If the child is older and arranges to meet a friend in town and she still hasn't arrived 20 minutes after the arranged time, she could call the friend's mobile phone or call her home, 'Hello, it's X. I'm calling because I arranged to meet Y at 11am in town and she hasn't arrived yet. Was she late leaving home? Did she say exactly where she's meeting me? There might have been a misunderstanding . . .'

Advice

Role plays

Ask for two volunteers, A and B. A is to ring B to invite him round for the day. Ask the class to help prepare A for the call.

A and B stand back to back. A makes the sound of a phone ringing, miming holding a handset, until B picks up and says hello. A is to say who she is and why she is calling.

Invite the class to comment on how well A and B understood one another and the reason for the call. Did A achieve a satisfactory outcome to the call?

Other role-play suggestions:

- A is to invite B swimming, going to meet in town first and then getting the bus back together for a meal at A's house.

- A is to invite B round with A's father being able to collect B but needing B's parents to take him back home.

- A is to invite B to go to the cinema on Saturday afternoon.

- A is to ask B if she can borrow an outfit for a fancy dress party at a relative's house.

- A is to ask B if he picked up her homework diary by mistake as she'd picked up B's. Could they swap tomorrow? (Repeat the role play with A and B's mum, 'Hello, is that Mrs X? It's A. I'm calling because I picked up B's homework diary by mistake. I only realized when I got home. I'm sorry. I was hoping that B might have my diary so that we could swap in school tomorrow.')

Receiving a telephone call

Learning to answer the telephone in a polite manner is an important social skill. For example, the child should say, 'Hello?' in a loud and clear voice and wait for the caller to identify himself and say who he wants to speak to.
If there's no one living at home with that name, the child should say, 'I think you have the wrong number.' If the caller wants to check that he punched in the numbers correctly he might ask the child what her number is but it is safer for the child to ask the caller the number he was hoping to get – then she can say that it differs from hers or that he has the right number for her phone but it isn't the number he needs to get hold of the person he wants to speak to.

If the caller names a member of the child's household to whom he wishes to speak, the child should say, 'I'll just get her. Who's calling please?' If that person is unavailable (for example, on the loo), she could say, 'Can I get her to call you back in ten minutes? She can't come to the phone at the moment.' However, if it's a close friend or relative who's calling, she could admit to the family member being on the loo without risk of embarrassment.

If the person the caller wants to speak to is out, the child should say, 'I'm sorry, she's out. Would you like to leave a message? Could you hold on a moment while I find a pen and paper?' Once she has found these items, she should say, 'OK, I've got the pen and paper. What's the message please?'
It is usual to repeat the message back to the caller to check for accuracy.

Discuss what children should do when answering the phone. (Saying, 'Yeah?' is not as polite as saying, 'Hello?' They mustn't pick up the receiver and say nothing – the caller won't realize there's anyone at the other end. Nor should they pick up the receiver and hang up immediately afterwards – it's rude.)

Role plays

Explain that you are going to be the caller. Each time the children hear you make the sound of a ringing phone they should put up their hands if they'd like to answer the call. When you point at someone, she (A) answers the call by saying, 'Hello?' You will be a different caller each time the phone rings.

After each call, discuss how it went and repeat the role play if necessary. Pay particular attention to the child's social safety and social graces. Here are some scenarios (depending on age, the child is either at home alone or with a babysitter):

- You ask to speak to A's mother to cancel your trip together tomorrow.

- You are A's friend. Invite her round after school tomorrow to play on your new Wii game.

- You are A's dad's work colleague and need to speak to him urgently about a work matter.

- Ask A where she lives without giving a name – you are a nasty caller. If A complies, ask more and more personal questions.

- You ask A to look for your glasses – you think you left them behind during a visit earlier in the day.

- You want to speak to A's dad to cancel meeting him after work tomorrow. As he's not in you'd like to leave a message.

When there's spare time at the end of a lesson you could role-play quick impromptu phone calls.

Awkward situations

The more embarrassing situations children are exposed to the more they can learn. It is only through making mistakes, or observing other people's mistakes, that they can understand what went wrong and why. Below are some potentially awkward situations for children, with suggestions of how to rescue the moment. These can be used in the role plays mentioned opposite.

Your mum cancelled a trip out with a friend saying she wasn't feeling well. Later that friend rings back to ask your mum something, but she's gone shopping. What do you say? (If you tell the truth, your mum's friend will feel hurt and your mum will feel embarrassed about being caught out in a lie; it might threaten their friendship. The most tactful thing to say is that she is in the bathroom and can't come to the phone. Then call your mum on her mobile to say what's happened.)

Your best friend tells you a big secret about another friend. Three weeks later that second friend tells you the secret. How do you behave? (You must not say, 'Oh, I already knew. X told me.' You must feign surprise so that you don't get your best friend into trouble or hurt your other friend's feelings by making her feel betrayed.)

A friend gives you a present for your birthday. When you unwrap it you find it is identical to one that your parents got you. What do you say and do? (You must not say, 'Oh, my dad's already got me one of those', as that will devalue the gift and hurt your friend's feelings, but instead say, 'Oh great. Thanks!' Explain the problem to your parents and secretly give one present away so that your friend won't ever know that you had two identical presents.)

Role plays

Explain each awkward scenario in turn to the class. Ask them what they should say and do if they were in that situation.

Ask for volunteers to act out each scene. Invite the class to comment and suggest ways to deal with the situation more skilfully. Ask the volunteers to re-enact the scene to show how it's done. Suggestions include:

- Your aunt tells you that the picture you drew is lovely. You disagree. What should you say and do? (Just say thank you and leave it at that.)

- Your elderly grandmother is very forgetful and asks you the same questions several times in a row, 'Where's your dad? When's he coming back? How do you like school? Do you have many friends?' What should you do or say? (Just keep answering the questions patiently – she can't help how she is.)

- Your aunt visits your house and gives a present to your sister. But it's your birthday, not hers. What do you do and say? (Don't say that it's your birthday. Show interest in your sister's present and admire it. Sort out feelings of disappointment and jealousy after your aunt has gone.)

- You hear that friends are throwing a surprise party for you. What do you do when you open the door and see all your friends (the rest of the class) shouting, 'Surprise'? (You should pretend that it really is a surprise. Even after the event, don't let on that you already knew to the organizers; it will make them feel disappointed that the surprise was spoilt and they will feel angry with the person who told you.)

Ask the children to suggest awkward scenarios from their own experiences to role-play.

5

Friendships

Why do we need friends?

Children need friends to play with, to be silly with, to have fun with, for company outside the home and in school, to go to clubs with, to talk to, to share problems with, to help one another, to keep one another safe and to play games that are meant for more than one person. Having friends also increases children's self-esteem as it shows that other people value them and their company, and allows children to practise their social skills so that they become better and better at being a friend as they grow up.

Friends are essential to a happy life; good friends are extremely precious and should be treasured. Many children take friends for granted – they have always had them and can't imagine life without them. However, other children aren't so lucky. They might make friends but keep falling out with them or they might never manage to make a friend and enviously regard those children who have got friends and wonder why they can't have friends too. Some children barge in on other friendship groups, eager to join in, but wonder why they are impatiently sent away. These things can be remedied. An understanding of what friends are for helps to clarify what kinds of behaviour will be valued by a hoped-for friend.

Advice

Friendships don't just happen, they have to be worked at. By understanding the social complexities of friendships children are better able to achieve a satisfying social network.

Discuss the following questions with the class:

- What are friends? (Other children you like, care about and enjoy being with. Usually they are of a similar age – although adult friendships can be much more diverse – and they have things in common with you so that you can enjoy doing similar things together. Friends are people you can share your thoughts and feelings with and discuss problems in your life with – and people you can celebrate with when things go well. Friends don't mind sharing things such as toys, DVDs and CDs.)

- What things do you do with your friends?

- Why do you need friends?

- What characteristics do you think friends should have? (Being fun, kind, helpful, sympathetic, relaxing to be with, honest, trustworthy, protective, loyal, tactful, sensitive.)

- Think about how good a friend you think you are. What things could you do to be a better friend? (Be more understanding and supportive, talk less and listen more, show you care, avoid unkind teasing.)

- Think about whether you value your friends. How could you show that you value them? (If they are ill, call them to find out how they are and perhaps visit them. Make them get well cards. Remember their birthdays. Notice if they don't look happy and ask what's wrong – don't be easily fobbed off – and show you genuinely care. Share your feelings in the hope that your friends will share theirs. Show pleasure in their company and say how much you appreciate the things they do for you. Be affectionate.)

Application

55

Judging too soon

Children can make up their minds in a few seconds of meeting whether they like someone or not. Sometimes they simply observe from afar and write off another person as someone they'd rather not get to know. Although it might only be a tiny movement, a particular expression, the physical appearance or the clothes the person is wearing that puts children off, the barriers they erect subconsciously can be hard to break down. If children are aware of how they can instantly dislike someone they might take more pains themselves in their social behaviour and be less quick to judge other people on theirs.

Sometimes a person appeals to children instantly for some reason. They might fulfil their expectations or they might find out a lot later that actually the person wasn't very pleasant to know after all and regret becoming so friendly with them. They might have learned to be more cautious in the future.

Advice

Activity

Ask the children to sit opposite a child they have not spoken to before and chat to find out about each other. They could talk about how big a family they have, whether they have any pets, what kind of music, television programmes and films they like, what sport they enjoy doing, whether they play a musical instrument, whether they have any hobbies and what their favourite colour, food or football teams are.

After ten minutes or so, ask the pairs to make groups of four. Each member of the pair should introduce their partner to the two newcomers and tell them what they have found out about the other person. This will show how well they have listened to what their partner said and will also stretch their reporting skills. Being articulate when talking to others is important, as communication is vital for building friendships.

Discuss the following questions with the class:

• Did you find that you had more things in common with the other children than you had expected?

• Had you made some incorrect assumptions about the other person?

• Have you ever made friends with someone you first disliked?

• Have you ever broken up with someone you'd taken an instant liking to?

• What have you learned about new relationships? (That you shouldn't discount becoming friendly towards someone just because you don't like the look of them or how they behave; other people can make incorrect assumptions about you. That even if you don't particularly like someone you probably have more things in common with each other than you expect.)

Making friends

Very young children can get away with simply saying, 'Would you like to play with me?' and, if the other child agrees, they have a new friend. But older children need to talk to determine whether they have anything in common and whether they find each other's company enjoyable. They also need to try to make a good impression, avoiding off-putting behaviour, such as snatching, being aggressive, showing off, swearing, picking their nose, spitting, making unkind comments, talking only about themselves and eating with poor table manners. Unless both children gain something from the new interaction, it is unlikely that either of them will ever want to meet up again.

If the initial meeting has gone well, the children might arrange to see each other again. However, getting to know each other needs to be done gradually. It takes time to get to know whether the other person can be trusted with very personal information or family secrets. So, in early conversations, children should concentrate on telling superficial information about themselves, such as where they go to school, what subjects they like and dislike and what sports they enjoy.

The children might arrange subsequent meetings as long as nothing off-putting happens in the meantime. Then the relationship becomes established and it is safer for children to divulge occasionally a little more about their personal life. Intimacy in a friendship can only be achieved if both children are prepared to give away a little more of their lives over time. If personal issues are never discussed, intimacy is limited. (Also see pages 68 and 69.)

Discuss how children can find out whether they might like to be friends with someone new and how friendships start.

Discuss barriers children might have that prevent a friendship forming or progressing.

Role play

Ask for two volunteers, A and B. A is a new pupil in the school, B is a pupil at the same school. They should sit opposite each other and chat while the class observes.

B could ask A where she came from, why she's changed schools, whether her last school was the same size as this one, her age, what games she likes to play, what music she likes to listen to and whether she has any pets, hobbies or special interests.

Below are suggested backgrounds for A – which can be embellished:

A (girl): Wanda's parents are divorced and their house had to be sold. They moved to a flat above a shop near her grandmother. Wanda loves all sport and has a brother at nursery.

A (boy): Aravindan's father was relocated through his job. Aravindan is not keen on football or rugby but enjoys playing chess. In his last school he sang in the choir and played the clarinet in the orchestra.

Discuss whether the conversation was balanced or whether only one child asked all the questions. Did it sound like an interrogation or was the conversation smooth and natural? If A asked a personal question of B, did A volunteer similar information without waiting to be asked? Doing this occasionally helps fluency in conversation.

Social networks

Social networks are made up of friends and acquaintances. Children who all socialize with one another very regularly such as a group of friends from school, from a club or from a religious group, form a clique. Cliques can be very useful when children need help in an emergency, as everyone knows about the problem at the same time. However, cliques are not good at keeping secrets – there's much temptation and opportunity to tell other clique members. Intimacy in cliques can be very high because the children frequently spend a great deal of time with one another.

Looser social networks comprise a more diverse group, such as a school friend, a neighbour, the child of a parent's friend and someone from a religious group – each child might know one other child from the group but only the core child will know everyone so any news will take much longer to get round. Intimacy tends to be less since children spread their time between friends, reducing the frequency of meeting individuals. However, secrets are better kept than with cliques.

When children socialize with one other child who does not mix with any other people in their social network that friend can be called an isolate – and anything said in confidence is unlikely to be shared with anyone else in that child's social network. To get the best of all types of friendship, it is good to have a mix of close-knit cliques, looser groups and isolates.

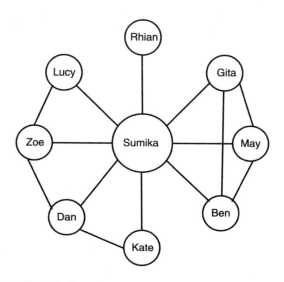

Advice

Use the diagram opposite to discuss the following questions with the class:

Sumika's social network is made up of an isolate (Rhian), a clique (Gita, May and Ben) and a looser social group (Kate, Dan, Zoe and Lucy).

- Apart from Sumika, who does Rhian know? (No one.) What is good about having an isolate as a friend?

- Who does May socialize with? (Gita, Ben and Sumika.) Does May usually socialize with these people at the same time? (Yes.)

- What are the advantages and disadvantages of a clique?

- Who does Lucy socialize with? (Sumika and Zoe.)

- Sumika tells Kate about a problem she needs help with. How would Lucy get to hear about it if she's not often in touch with Sumika? (Through Kate telling Dan, Dan telling Zoe, and Zoe telling Lucy.) Is this a quick way of Lucy finding out that Sumika's in trouble? (No – there might be a gap of a week or more between each 'intermediary' meeting up.) If Dan didn't know Sumika, would the news still reach Lucy? (Probably – Dan would be aware that Zoe knows Sumika so would pass on news about Sumika from Kate to Zoe. Zoe would then mention the news to Lucy the next time they met.) What does this tell you about friends keeping secrets? (Know who is friendly with whom before you confide – as well as waiting for trust to build up on both sides.)

- What are the advantages and disadvantages of a looser knit social group?

- Does the size of your social network determine whether you feel lonely?

- What can you do if you feel lonely? (Try to identify why. Try to make more friends, increase the frequency of meeting friends and increase intimacy with existing friends.)

Maintaining friendships

Once the work of establishing a friendship is done, children still need to make an effort to keep that friendship going. Friendships can stagnate through a lack of intimacy and through an apparent lack of interest in either party. There needs to be continued contact where each friend contacts the other roughly the same amount of times – which is hard if one friend wants much more contact than the other wants, or is prepared, to give. This can lead to disappointment in the child who wants frequent contact and irritation in the child who wants only occasional contact. Here are some dos and don'ts:

Do	Don't
Look and sound pleased to see them.	Boast.
Show you enjoy their company (by, for example, laughing or hugging).	Show jealousy.
Face people when you speak to them, or when they speak to you, and look them in the eye.	Break confidences – unless it is to protect your friend.
Share the joy of any successes and commiserate with disappointments – show that you care.	Tell lies.
Be prepared to lend things.	Spread rumours.
Notice when they look upset and ask what's wrong.	Hurt or bully.
Be interested in them – don't just talk about yourself.	Ignore them when you are with other people.
Share information about your life – let them get to know you.	Stop them from seeing other friends or going out with other people: even best friends don't own each other.
Be prepared to have physical contact – at least, when they are upset.	Be brutally honest or untactful.
Be prepared to compromise when you disagree (see page 86).	Fail to stick up for your friend in their absence if someone's being unfair about them.

Discuss the following questions with the class:

- What do you like about your friends?

- What sort of things help to keep your friendship going? (Young children might support one another by going in pairs to ask their teacher a question if they are nervous about going alone. Older children might give advice on how a friend looks or on how to improve their ball skills.)

- What things have damaged your friendships? (Being called names, being shunned, having your successes ignored, being made fun of for getting something wrong.)

- Spend a few moments thinking privately about whether you've hurt your friends. Help make up a class list of dos and don'ts for friendships.

- What makes a child popular? (Being polite, fun to be with, jokey, confident, outgoing, attractive, sporty, all-inclusive and protecting others from being bullied in any way – and smiling a great deal.)

- What characteristics make a child unpopular? (Being impolite, dirty and smelly, shy, unconfident, a 'swot' – showing off about academic achievement can make a child prone to being bullied.)

- A lack of self-awareness prevents people from monitoring their own behaviour and checking any provocative or hostile comments or acts. How self-aware are you? Can you identify any shortcomings in yourself, such as being irritating, unkind or provocative? How would you feel if someone says or does the things to you that you say or do to someone else?

- How could you work on the characteristics that others find appealing? (Learn from other people's successful relationships. Filter your thoughts to stop you saying something you might regret. Ask yourself, would you like that said or done to you? Think, 'If I don't have something good to say about someone, perhaps I shouldn't say it at all.')

Application

False friends

False friends only pretend to be good friends. They might become friendly with someone because there isn't anyone else who would put up with them. They might want something from that person – such as money or gossip – that can be traded to inveigle their way into other, more prized, friendship groups, or they might have poor social skills and so do not understand the havoc they wreak.

A false friend says unkind things behind a child's back, says things to make them feel small, teases nastily, makes fun of them, spreads rumours about them, gossips about them, leaves them out of games, refuses to share things, copies from them and makes out the work was theirs, uses them by being nice only when it suits them or when they want something from them.

It can be hard to detect false friends – some people take a while to show what they are truly like and it can take time for children to listen to their instincts that tell them someone is not good for them. They should question whether they would do to a friend what's been done to them and whether the 'friend' makes them feel good about themselves. When dealing with false friends, children should use confident – not aggressive – body language and shouldn't say anything to incite the false friend's anger.

Advice

Discuss the following questions with the class:

- What is a 'false friend'?

- How can you identify a false friend? (By the way that friend makes you feel. Good friends apologize, explain hurtful behaviour and say they won't do it again.)

- What kinds of things do false friends do?

- Have you had experience of false friends? What happened? What did you do about them? (Did you point out to them that they'd been unkind or had betrayed you? Did you try to get your own back or did you ignore them?)

- When is it a good time to end the relationship? (When you feel hurt on a regular basis and despite trying to right the situation, it has continued, or if the person has physically harmed you in some way. Leaving things as they are should not be considered as that allows the false friend to continue bullying behaviour unchecked.)

Role play

Ask for two volunteers, A and B. They are to role-play a situation that has happened to them – or someone they know – where the child who was hurt (B) talks to the false friend (A).

A: Says or does the nasty thing.

B: 'What you just said (or did) was very hurtful to me. It seemed to me that you did it on purpose. That's not what friends are for. If you don't stop hurting my feelings I won't want to be friends with you any more.' (It is very important to have a penalty so that the false friend knows what will happen if they don't change their ways.)

6 Making conversation

Conversation rules

Like games, conversations have rules. And, like games, if children don't know the rules, or don't stick to them, other people won't warm to them or seek their company. Here are some conversation rules:

Do	Don't
Show interest in the other person – be prepared to ask questions.	Interrupt someone already speaking – unless it's an emergency.
Match the other person's mood. If they are sad, speak softly and sound sympathetic.	Hog the conversation – it needs to be balanced between the two people involved.
Try to introduce humour.	Look bored or say that you've heard it all before.
Pause every so often to allow the other person to contribute.	Finish the other person's sentence for them – unless they obviously need help.
Talk about feelings – yours and the other person's.	Try to change the subject unless the other person looks as if they've said all they want to say about it.
Chat about a variety of subjects not just one that interests you – unless the other person is equally interested in the subject.	Give too much information away about yourself too early, before you know whether you can trust that person.

Many children, although eager to make friends, don't know how to start or keep a conversation going and may fall foul of one or more conversation rules. They can also find it hard to talk about emotions.

Activity 1

Discuss how conversation works and ask the class to think up dos and don'ts for rewarding conversation.

Activity 2

Explain the use of a 'talking stick', where only the person holding the stick is allowed to speak. Ask the class to divide into pairs. Each pair should find a pen or pencil to act as their talking stick while they are in conversation. When each child finishes what they want to say they should pass the talking stick to their partner.

After a few minutes ask the class how they found the exercise. What was the point of the exercise? (To show that they should take it in turns to speak and not interrupt when someone else is speaking.)

Did the children try to keep the conversation on the same subject lines as at the start of the conversation or did they have a shift of conversation connected to the original one in some way? Were there more shifts in conversation where each one was connected to the one before it?

Discuss what children should do if they want to join a group of people already talking. (Stand close enough to the group to be noticed. Follow the conversation and only contribute when there is a pause in the conversation. Don't try to take over the conversation of the whole group by starting to talk about something completely different; it has to be connected.)

Activity 3

Ask the class to divide into threes. Two out of the three children start a conversation with each other. The third person of each group must skilfully join the conversation. How did they manage it?

Application

Self-disclosure

When children self-disclose they reveal things about themselves, such as their thoughts, opinions, fears, hopes, feelings and experiences. However, if very personal information is disclosed too easily it can put others off from being friendly and children risk being judged. They also risk their secrets being gossiped about which might lay them open to being bullied. Children should also be wary of disclosing unkind thoughts about another child to someone they don't know well – this person might socialize with the child mentioned so might tell them what was said – and they might retaliate.

There is no set time at which it is safe to self-disclose to friends – it is a matter of personal judgement. However, children should avoid mentioning in early conversations that, for example, their dad is in prison, their mother is an alcoholic, they have had a pregnancy terminated or they have a major problem of some kind (unless the problem is very obvious – then the child needs to explain to get understanding and acceptance). These kinds of revelations should be saved for further down the line if the relationship survives the first few meetings. Even then, only a little should be given away at once. A child becoming closer to someone should wait to see how they react to what is said and whether they also divulge personal information at the same level.

Very sensitive information – that children would feel afraid of everyone knowing and would make them feel very hurt if their friends were not to keep it a secret – should be held back until any relationship is well established and the friends have proved themselves trustworthy.

Advice

Discuss what initial conversations should be about: exchanging superficial information such as where children are from (without giving the actual address), how old they are, what games they like to play, what music they like to listen to, and whether they have siblings, pets, hobbies or special interests. This kind of information could be rated at level 1.

Activity

Ask the children to make a poster of the kinds of things about themselves that they wouldn't mind other people knowing – ensuring that higher level information is not included.

Discuss what kinds of things children might not mind close friends knowing after three months or so of an uninterrupted friendship where trust has not been broken. They should consider this information at level 2. (Suggestions include: their parents separating or divorcing, their older brother being diagnosed with cancer, their mum needing surgery, feeling unhappy about their appearance, feeling desperate to have a boyfriend/girlfriend.)

Discuss what kinds of things might be classed as level 3 information – such as they would only give away to a best friend after years of friendship. (Suggestions include: they are unhappy at home, they are worried about one of their parents dying, they have been abused, their dad has a severe mental illness, they once tried to kill themselves, they think they might be gay or pregnant or have a sexually transmitted infection.)

Beginnings and endings

When children meet someone new for the first time it can be hard to think of something to say so it is good to consider what subject areas they should touch on – and what is taboo. (Also see page 58.) Questions they should not touch on include: 'How much do your parents earn?' 'What's your house worth?' 'Have you had sex?' 'Are you gay?'

When children are meeting someone they have met before, the conversation can get off to an easier start if they can recall the main elements of the previous conversation to join the last conversation with the new one. For example, if a child mentioned he was playing in a football match against another school, they could ask how that match went.

Saying goodbye can be hard – who will do it first? (See page 44.) It is important for children to say goodbye – not just walk off – and, if possible, add something to make the ending seem less hurried and 'neater', such as, 'I hope your next match goes just as well!' And, if they've only just met the other person, they could say, 'I enjoyed talking to you' or, 'I enjoyed meeting you.'

There can be awkward moments when children are in a shop or in the street and see someone they recognize but don't have time to stop to chat. Should they try to sneak by without being noticed – which could offend the other person if they notice them? Or should they say hello and walk briskly by – which could also offend? It is far better to acknowledge the other person but to be upfront about being short of time. Forewarning the other person makes them more understanding about an abrupt departure.

Remind the children about things they can talk about when meeting someone for the first time (see page 68).

Role play 1

Ask for two volunteers, A and B, who are in the same year at school but in different classes. They have never talked to each other before. They must strike up a conversation. After about three minutes the bus arrives at school. A and B must skilfully end their conversation. Discuss how the role play went. It can be repeated with improvements.

Discuss how to start a conversation with someone they have met before. Is there a way of joining the last conversation to the new one to increase the feeling of connection?

The same volunteers, A and B, are to sit together on the bus the next day. They must greet each other and join up the last conversation with this one. Discuss how it went and what improvements could be made.

Role play 2

Discuss a way of smoothing leave-taking when children meet someone by chance and they know they don't have long to talk before they must leave.

Ask for two volunteers, A and B, to role-play a chance meeting in the street where one of them has little time to chat. Suggestion:

A: 'Hi. How are you?/What are you doing here? I can't stay for long as I've got to catch a bus.'

B: 'What time does it go?'

A: 'Ten to. I've got five minutes. So, how are things?'

Listening

Some children talk at each other, rather than listening to what another child is saying and then responding to it. They might be so engrossed in what they want to say that they totally discount the other child's need to talk about something important in their life. Conversations like this are one way and unrewarding to the listener. However, mainly one-way conversations are expected when a friend is in trouble and needs to explain what has gone wrong. Then the listener can sympathize, give emotional support and perhaps think up some practical suggestions to help.

During conversation children need to show that they are paying attention by making noises such as, 'Mm', 'Oh?', 'Really?', 'No!', 'Never!', by nodding, by not fidgeting and by making plenty of eye contact.

Sometimes understanding can be limited, so children can check what was said, 'Your teacher said what to you?' or delve deeper, 'Do you think he was being mean deliberately?' Active listening, like this, is very rewarding to the speaker because it shows interest.

Although it is sometimes boring to listen to someone else talk, children must learn to feign interest so as not to offend. If they take the trouble to listen carefully to what someone else has to say, that person is more likely to take pains to listen to them when they have something important to impart too. If these social niceties aren't observed, it is more likely that children won't be able to keep friends – no one will think they are interested in them – and they could end up lonely.

Advice

Discuss the following questions with the children:

- What things show that someone is listening?
- How would you show that you are bored and can't wait to get away? (Look at your watch, look over the speaker's shoulder or around the room, yawn, look at the floor, fidget with your clothes.) Try to hide your boredom so you don't offend.

Role play

Ask for two volunteers, A and B. A arrives late as her house was burgled the evening before. B is sitting next to A in a lesson where chatting is allowed. A is only to give explanations when B asks questions to prompt her. The questions B chooses are carefully chosen through listening to what A says. For example:

B: 'Why are you late?'

A: 'We were burgled last night.'

B: 'Burgled? Never! What happened?'

A: 'Well, we'd gone to my nan's. When we got home we found a smashed window.'

B: 'Is that how they got in?'

A: 'No. They used the hole to get the back door open.'

B: 'So they smashed the kitchen window?'

A: 'Yes. There was glass everywhere.'

B: 'What was taken?'

A: 'The TV, DVD player, my Wii . . .'

B: 'Not your Wii? What about your games? Did they take them too?'

Application

73

Building rapport

When children have good rapport with someone they have a strong mutual feeling of connection – they are on the same 'wavelength'. They like each other, they understand each other, they are interested in each other and they care about each other. They might have much in common, care about the same kinds of things and have similar life values. Although such a high level of rapport usually exists between best friends, children can start to build rapport with complete strangers.

For example, two children are waiting outside the head of year's office. They might share the same feelings of trepidation, but no rapport can develop until one child looks at, or speaks to, the other. They might smile at each other or one might exaggerate trembling hands to show he or she is nervous and the other might copy the action or smile. Or the children might talk: 'What are you here for?' 'Got sent out of class.' 'Me too.' Immediately, they have something in common and are bound by their shared misdemeanours. Being aware of thoughts and feelings (and beliefs and values) helps children to identify with like-minded people for immediate rapport and for the foundation of a new friendship.

Sometimes body language shows when two children have rapport – unconsciously one child crosses their ankles to copy another child. Socially skilled people deliberately copy body posture to increase the feeling of rapport between them and the person with whom they are interacting. This can be done for positive reasons (to make friends or to be an effective counsellor) or negative reasons (to increase someone's confidence in them so that they can con them).

Discuss what it means when there is rapport between two people. What kinds of things help to develop rapport? Suggestions include:

- Facing each other squarely with feet facing forwards (so that it doesn't look as if you want to run away).

- Leaning towards each other.

- Having a similar body posture.

- Making plenty of eye contact.

- Sharing a joke, or taking sips from a drink at the same time.

- Having an open posture – spreading out rather than being in a tight ball or having your arms folded.

- Showing you are paying attention by nodding and by avoiding fidgeting.

- Copying the speed and tone of the person who speaks: if they speak fast and loud you might speak fast and loud too – unless they are angry and you are trying to calm them down.

- Using the same key words as the other person. For example, saying that's 'cool' rather than that's 'great'. You might swear to match the other person's swearing even if you don't do it at home – just to help you fit in.

- Avoiding deliberately pronouncing a word differently just to get 'one up' on the other person.

- Saying what you think of something or how you feel or whether you agree with the other person.

- Allowing the other person to have their turn at talking – and being prepared to have some silences.

- Playing down differences between you and emphasizing commonalities.

Role play

Ask for two volunteers, A and B, to role-play waiting outside the head of year's office to be disciplined. Can they build rapport between them? Invite the class to comment – what improvements could be made? Repeat the role play to show a more skilful approach.

Building empathy

Empathy is the ability to perceive, recognize and feel the emotion of another person as though their situation were happening to you – to put yourself 'in the other person's shoes'. To empathize with someone, children need to understand and respect them, value their beliefs, accept their life values and feel their feelings.

When children are sympathetic they merely express sorrow that the other person is in trouble – they don't necessarily imagine how it would feel being that other person. Being sympathetic, as well as empathetic, makes children more effective in their relationships.

When empathy is lacking, children need to help the other person understand by describing their feelings – something which many children find hard to do, particularly boys. When dealing with conflict, children need to show they are empathetic to negotiate successfully (see page 86).

For example, if a girl says that she is having a hard time the friend should not say, 'You think you've got it hard? What about me . . .', but accept what she says and ask to understand more about the situation, 'What's the matter?' After the explanation, the friend should not say something dismissive such as, 'Oh, that happened to me ages ago. It's no big deal', but accept that the girl's experience could be different from hers or that the girl might not be as resilient as her.

When teachers empathize with children in their class, they help contribute to a positive learning environment and encourage children to empathize with one another – which helps to reduce bullying. Empathetic bystanders in a bullying situation are more likely to intervene to help the victim, making the bully far more likely to stop. Silence from bystanders is viewed by bullies as tacit encouragement. (See also pages 102 to 105.)

Advice

Discuss the following questions with the class:

- What is the difference between empathy and sympathy?

- When might it be good to show empathy? (When someone is hurt, physically or emotionally; when someone is being bullied or feels sad about something.)

- How do you think people feel when a much-loved pet dies? (Sad, missing the animal, lonely, afraid of something similar happening to them or to someone they love.)

- What could you do to help if your friend's grandfather dies? (Say, 'I'm sorry. I'd miss my grandad loads if he died. It must be awful for you.' Give her a card or a little present to cheer her up and be especially kind to her. Invite her to talk about what happened and relate happy memories of the deceased.)

Ask the children to 'put themselves in their friend's shoes' by imagining what they might feel when:

- Her bus money has been stolen. (Angry at the thief, scared about getting into trouble at home for not taking better care of her money, fearful of how she's going to get home.)

- Someone stamped on her sandwiches. (Angry, upset, hungry, scared that it might happen again.)

- A teacher shouted at her for talking – but she was helping you with your work. (Hurt, feeling the teacher was not being fair, angry, misunderstood, embarrassed by everyone looking at her, let down if you didn't stand up for her.)

- The class has been invited to a birthday party – but she's not allowed to go. (Embarrassment, shame, angry with her parents, left out.)

- She has a learning disability. Classmates call her stupid and laugh behind her back. (Feeling bad about herself, ashamed, embarrassed, dreading coming to school, fearing being laughed at again, lonely and without friends.)

7

Getting on with others

Teamwork

A team is a group of people working together cooperatively to achieve the same goal. To work successfully in a team, children need to:

- question the task and discuss the best way to go about it
- show respect to all team members and allow each member to have their say
- make collective decisions and ensure that everyone participates – otherwise it won't be a team effort
- take any concerns a team member may have seriously
- explain why they want to reject an idea – and praise good ideas
- share thoughts to encourage other team members to share theirs
- be constructive if they must criticize
- monitor their motives before they criticize. Would they still criticize if the person was someone they liked better?
- avoid being bossy, and be prepared to accept criticism
- share equipment and allow everyone to have their turn
- cooperate with other members – give help when they need it
- concentrate on the task given and avoid conflict
- communicate clearly so that everyone understands what they are doing and why and what difficulties have to be overcome
- be quick to apologize if they have done something wrong – and be prepared to forgive others their mistakes.

Advice

No one can operate as a single entity – everyone has to rely on other people for something. The better children get on with others, the happier and more successful they become.

Discuss what a team is.

Activity 1

Help the children to build up a list of rules a team should have to make it work well. Discuss the following questions with the class:

- Sometimes, when working in groups, the same child always takes charge. What could change in the way a lesson is run so that other children get a chance to take the lead? (Mixing groups can break the cycle of the same child being the 'boss'.)

- What could you do about a team member who doesn't participate? (Invite that person to contribute, 'What do you think, Tamara?')

- Do you think you have the skills to be a team player? If you feel you are lacking in skills, how could you gain these skills? (By practising listening and cooperating with other people – friends, parents, siblings and teachers.)

Activity 2

Ask the children to form groups of around six. Give them a task to solve as a team, such as devising a scheme to:

- tackle bullying in school
- prevent litter-dropping and graffiti in school
- raise money for a good cause.

Discuss how well the team operated. Did someone direct the other team members and help to keep them focused? If so, did they abuse their power by taking over or did they use it to ensure everyone was included and respected? What team skills did they use? What could have been improved? Would the children be prepared to carry out the suggestions they came up with?

Application

79

Exploring anger

Anger is a very strong emotion where one child feels antagonistic or hostile towards another. It is frequently viewed as a negative emotion because it can be so destructive, but sometimes it can be very positive to express anger.

For anger to be addressed in a positive way it should cause no harm to the child, to another person or to property. Feelings should be talked about – or shouted about if the occasion merits it. Expressing anger appropriately clears the air and helps to repair misunderstandings and failures in relationships. When relationships are repaired after a rift they become stronger as each person has reached a new understanding and renegotiated boundaries. Good things about children displaying anger are that they relieve their frustration, they let their anger 'burn out' and they show the other person that they are hurting inside.

Bad things about children displaying anger are that it increases aggression between them and other people that could result in serious injury or even death. They might feel foolish for losing control. If they take out their anger on themselves they could be seriously harmed, they could become depressed or they might become addicted to bad habits, eating patterns or drink or drugs – and they might be lonely and without friends. If children take out their anger on objects they might damage something they, or someone close to them, value – and they might damage themselves while doing it. They could even be arrested and end up with a police record. And their behaviour won't have solved the original problem.

Advice

Discuss the following questions with the class:

- What is anger?

- How do people show that they are angry? (Through verbal abuse, physical abuse and self-harm, by starving themselves, overeating, under-eating, drinking, taking illegal drugs, solvent-sniffing, stealing, isolating themselves and withdrawing from social contact, and through vandalism.)

- Should anger be expressed or repressed? (Repressing anger causes angry feelings to build up until it affects the people you live and study with and your ability to feel happy and to concentrate. Bottled up feelings can make you behave in an inappropriate way, making an exaggerated response to a small event and getting it out of proportion. You might also unfairly take out your problems on someone close to you or even yourself through self-harming behaviour.)

- What are the good things about showing anger?

- What are the bad things about showing anger?

- What kind of things make people feel angry? (People become angry when they are treated unfairly or are tormented in some way, when something has been done deliberately to hurt them physically or emotionally and when they are trapped – such as in a bullying situation. Some people seem to have anger as a character trait and are irritable much of the time – this is often described as having a 'short fuse'.)

- When would it be appropriate to get angry? (In situations where anyone would be angry – such as when you find out that your friend has betrayed you.)

Dealing with anger

Below is some advice to give to children.

When you are angry:

- Don't do anything immediately – leave the situation or count from one to ten before responding.
- Avoid the temptation to hurt the other person back, either physically or emotionally.
- Keep calm and check the facts.
- Focus on what you want.
- Rationalize. Have you done anything to upset the other person? Perhaps they have problems at home?
- Say how you feel about what was said or done and ask for an apology or a promise to make amends in some way. Have a penalty ready, such as not being prepared to do them another favour if they are not prepared to change.

When someone is angry with you:

- Suggest you meet up later to talk things through once they have had a chance to cool down. Focus on solutions.
- Try to find common ground on which you can agree on something.
- Show that you understand their point of view – which helps to calm them down. They will feel that you have listened to what they have to say and are taking the situation seriously.
- Calmly explain what you disagree with and why.
- Accept only the blame that is yours – reject the rest and explain why they are mistaken.
- Allow them time to think and to respond to each thing you say.
- Be prepared to meet them halfway.
- Take care over your safety. If the person is being abusive or offensive, walk away. Your safety is more important than scoring points.

If your friend is angry with someone else, keep calm to help them keep calm. Discourage an unconsidered reaction. Discuss how best to handle the situation.

Advice

Discuss the following questions with the class:

- When have you felt angry? How did you express your anger? Was this a good way of expressing it?

- Have you ever said or done things that you later regretted? What did you do about it? (You should always try to make amends – by apologizing for your anger and by talking calmly about what happened.)

- What strategies could you use to calm yourself down before you respond to the behaviour that made you angry?

- What strategies could you use to calm someone down if they are angry with you?

- How could you help an angry friend keep control of destructive behaviour?

Activity

Divide the children into pairs. Ask them to talk about a time when they got angry. Did their anger get them the outcome they'd hoped for?

Role play

Invite a pair of children, A and B, to role-play a situation they've just discussed. A is to be the angry child. For example:

A: 'You lied to me, you ****. I'm through with you! I hate you and I hope you go to hell!'

B: 'That's great! Just **** off!'

Invite the rest of the class to comment. Ask A and B to repeat the role play showing how A could have managed the situation better. For example:

A: 'When I rang you to ask if you'd come swimming with me you said you couldn't because your dad was taking you out. So I decided to go shopping in town instead. And I saw you with Sasha. Can you explain?'

B: 'I was going with Dad but he couldn't pick me up as his car broke down. I tried to ring you back but you'd already left. Then Sasha rang and invited me out with her so I went.'

Swearing

When children use a word or phrase to be abusive, aggressive, irreligious or irreverent towards someone, they are swearing. Many children use the words out of habit and don't know what they mean.

In primary schools children might swear for effect, to get someone's attention or to shock, or use swearing as a weapon by saying something another child does not understand – even when they don't understand it themselves. They might repeat words heard at home or they might copy other people's way of dealing with anger and frustration by saying and doing things these people have said and done.

It is important for children in secondary school to understand the words they use as this is part of taking responsibility for their behaviour. A letter home can enlighten parents as to the value of the lesson and could ask parents to consider their use of language at home – and the television programmes they allow their children to watch, as some expressions children use are taken directly from particular shows.

In secondary schools it is often enough for children to know the meaning of a word for them to decide not to use it. Other children might use the words out of habit – they have been using them for so long that it has become natural for them despite them being more effective if only used sparingly. Or they might use certain words to appear 'cool', to be one of the group or to show aggression – indicating they have power over other people. However, many children feel hurt and scared being in an environment where swearing is the norm. (See also page 133.)

Please note: children with Tourette's syndrome often use expletives uncontrollably and should in no way be judged negatively by peers or staff.

Discuss the following questions with the class:

- What is swearing? Give examples. Do you know what these words mean? (Primary children could just be asked to put swear words into categories of mild, strong and very offensive.)

- How do you feel about people who frequently swear?

- Some children come from families that don't use swear words. How do you think they feel being with people who do swear? (Might they feel frightened? If swear words are used on them, might they feel upset or hurt?)

- Why do some families swear and others don't? (All families have their own way of communicating. Some parents have made a conscious decision not to swear because they are religious. Others don't swear or allow their children to swear because they believe it is not the right way to talk to other people – it does not show respect for the other person and it makes them feel bad inside. Swearing also increases anger between people.)

- Have you ever repeatedly been sworn at for something? Did that make you feel angry? Did it make you feel good about yourself?

- Does it matter if children swear in school? Does it teach children to respect one another? Does it scare the younger children? Does it teach children positive ways of dealing with anger and frustration? Have you been bullied by children using swear words? How did that feel? Is school an appropriate place for swearing?

- Would you like to have a ban on swearing? (See page 133.) Some schools are successfully tackling swearing by giving wrist bands to pupils who pledge not to swear. You could consider alternative ways of communicating. For example, instead of being abusive if someone upsets you, you could say, 'Why did you do that?'

Conflict and negotiation

A child is in conflict with someone when they want something different to the other person or have opposing views. If neither party is prepared to give way, both have a situation of total conflict – and both lose. When neither person gets what they want, there is the risk of high conflict bringing anger and aggression into the relationship.

If a child gives in to the other person, the other person 'wins' – while they lose out. Sometimes it is not worth the effort for them to stand their ground. However, if one child always capitulates they will be seen as passive and others will take advantage of them. This lowers self-esteem since they don't stick up for their own needs and they are rarely, if ever, met.

The ideal is a situation where each child listens to the other, understands each other's needs and each is prepared to meet the other halfway to find an acceptable compromise so that they both can 'win' – they both get something they want out of the situation and neither of them feels as though the other has got the better of them. Negotiating to find an acceptable compromise is being assertive – each child recognizes and respects the other person's needs while not discounting their own.

If high conflict already exists between a child and another person, the child should try to keep calm and avoid antagonizing the other person. They should work out which things they can both agree on to show that they are taking the other person's concerns seriously, then decide on which things they are prepared to compromise and on which things they want to stand their ground – not quibbling over things that are unimportant.

Advice

Discuss the following questions with the class:

- What is meant by conflict?

- When have you been in a situation of conflict? What happened? How did the situation get resolved? Was it the outcome you hoped for? Was it a fair outcome? If not, what would have been a fair outcome?

- What would happen if the two people in conflict were not prepared to change the way they see the situation or to change what they insist upon?

- How could a situation of conflict be made fair? Can one person manage this on their own, or do both people have to try to make it fair? (Both.)

Explain how to reduce conflict by agreeing on some things and by negotiating others – and the need to stick to only what is high priority.

Role play

Invite two children, A and B, to have a disagreement about where they should go at the weekend. A always ends up choosing where to go but B wants to choose where to go this week. How will they sort it out? For example:

A: 'Let's go bowling on Saturday.'

B: 'I'd like to go to the cinema. There's a film I've been longing to see.'

A: 'Nah. Let's go bowling.'

B: 'I know you like to choose where to go, and that's been fine. But this week I'd really like to choose.'

A: 'Go to the cinema with someone else. Come bowling with me.'

B: 'It's fairer to take it in turns to decide how we spend our time.'

A: 'OK. My choice next week then?'

If A was not willing to compromise and B insisted on choosing, they would end up in conflict and they would have to go out alone or with other people instead.

Being genuine

When children want to convey an important message to someone because, for example, that person is upset and they want to assure them that they are sincere in their desire to help, it is vital that their body language upholds the verbal message they want to give – or their sincerity will be doubted and they could lose the other person's trust and friendship.

Not appearing to mean what they say could also land children in trouble with teachers – or with an employer. If they are asked to say sorry for a misdemeanour but apologize in such a manner as to suggest that they are insincere or even poking fun at the people who demand or deserve the apology, children are likely to get into more trouble – and suffer long-term dislike by the person concerned.

When children say sorry, they need to look the other person in the eye and maintain eye contact throughout their apology. The face needs to look serious without the glimmer of a smile and the voice needs to sound sad – at having made a mistake and having hurt the other person's feelings. It also needs to sound firm, to show they truly mean they are sorry. When the apology is over – and hopefully accepted – they need to keep a serious expression on their face. If they immediately turn away from the person they've just apologized to and smile at a friend – or worse, snigger – their apology will have been wasted and the other person won't trust what they say again.

Children should think carefully about their body language when they want to convey a message in earnest to have the best chance of mending rifts in relationships and to ensure that they are respected and trusted.

Advice

Explain the importance of displaying body language to match the words used.

Role plays

Ask for volunteers, A and B, to act out each of the following scenarios. Give A and B slips of paper with their scripts on. However, if B does not need a script, only tell A what to say. Discuss how genuine B seems.

A has won a competition

A (rushing up to B): 'Hey! Guess what! Remember that essay I entered for the competition? It came first! I've won a gift token!'

B: 'Well done! That's great!' (Looking and sounding genuinely pleased and excited for A. Girls could hug, boys could grasp the other's arm or pat his shoulder if they don't want to give a bear hug.)

A's grandmother has died

A (looking sad): 'My nana died on Saturday.'

B: 'Oh, I'm so sorry. That must be dreadful for you. No wonder you look sad. What happened?' (Looking and sounding concerned. Girls could hug, boys could place a hand on the other's shoulder.)

A wants to tell B a secret

A: 'If I tell you, you must promise not to tell anyone else.'

B: 'I promise. I'll keep it secret.' (Looking earnest and sounding firm and confident, maintaining eye contact throughout.)

A accuses B of stealing something

A: 'I don't believe you didn't steal my fountain pen.'

B: 'Honest! I wouldn't lie to you. I really didn't take it.' (Looking earnest, sounding firm and sincere, maintaining eye contact and displaying no shifty or nervous body language.)

Application

Discrimination

Discrimination is when a person deals less favourably with someone because of prejudice and/or stereotyping. *Prejudice* is when a person has a preconceived opinion on whether they like something, or someone, which is not based on fact. *Stereotyping* is when a person gives a fixed or exaggerated description about people from a particular group and applies it to individuals without exception. Stereotypes can become fixed in children's minds so that they are eventually considered factual despite there being evidence to the contrary.

There are many kinds of discrimination. Being ageist is discriminating against someone because of their age. A group of boys together on a street corner might be discriminated against when people decide they are up to no good or are part of a violent gang without having anything on which to found their suspicions. Job-seekers over 40 or 50 might be discriminated against by employers actively seeking young people to train and ignoring the experience of more mature employees. Elderly people might be discriminated against because they are vulnerable and need a lot of care.

Sex discrimination is treating women as second rate or inferior to men – or vice versa. Typically, women do not tend to get promoted to the same levels as men and do not earn as much when they are doing comparable work. Some transgendered people (who have had a sex change) can also be discriminated against, socially and at work.

People are also discriminated against on the grounds of their religion, colour, culture, language, race, social status, class, size (being very short or tall, or very fat or thin) and whether they have a mental or physical disability. Sometimes organizations try to reverse negative discrimination by deliberately seeking to employ more women, say, in engineering or black people in predominantly white institutions.

Discuss the following questions with the class:

- What is discrimination? Give examples.

- How does it feel to be discriminated against? Imagine how you would feel if everyone with a navy bag had to stay behind after school every day to clean the classrooms and pick up litter.

- How do we become discriminatory? (Accepting, without questioning, learned behaviour from family and friends as the norm.)

- If you saw a boy spitting in the street, would you assume all boys spit in the street? If someone tells you that his younger sister loves olives, would you assume that all younger sisters love olives? What does this tell you about how you should think about people, and the dangers that can occur if you don't think in this way? (You need to consider everyone as an individual and find out for yourself whether something said about someone else is true or you risk stereotyping.)

Activity

Ask the children to sit next to someone they've never sat next to before, or who they don't know well. Without talking, they should write down what kind of music, colours and food they think the other likes, and how they like to spend their free time. Were they right about each other? Can they sum people up in this way? (No!)

Challenge

Ask the children to spend the day with the person they don't know well, concentrating on commonalities rather than differences. At the end of the day, have they made a new friend?

Racism

Racism is believing that one race is superior to other races; the belief is fed by prejudice and stereotyping (see page 90). When children hear racist remarks at home they take them as fact and repeat what was said in the playground, sharing racism with their classmates. Racism is also perpetuated by listening to – and passing on – racist jokes. Being racist is being abusive, biased, a bully, ignorant, intolerant, narrow-minded, bigoted, blinkered and prejudiced. Racist people can also be dangerous as they can spread hatred and incite violence. 'Inciting racial hatred' is a criminal offence. Any racist behaviour, such as verbal abuse, harassment or physical violence, is also against the law.

To stop racism, children shouldn't laugh at racist jokes or pass them on. If someone makes a negative comment about someone from another ethnic group they should ask what they based their comment on. If there's no evidence to back up the comment, they should point it out or ask the person to take back what they said and apologize. Children need to look beyond external appearances and base their liking on personalities and commonalities. They should celebrate the rich culture brought to their area, enjoy the different music available to listen to and the range of foodstuffs available to eat. They could find out about other cultures by talking to people from those cultures and they could try to understand how other people's lives differ from theirs. They should build bridges rather than break them.

It is important to stop racism since hatred against a particular race can escalate and through increasing violence someone could be badly injured or even killed – or victims might be so unhappy they commit suicide.

Advice

Discuss the following questions with the class:

- What is racism? How do people become racist?
- Think of words to describe racist people.
- Is racism legal?
- How do you think it feels to be picked on because of your race? (It could make you feel valueless, scared, lacking in confidence and self-esteem. You might find it hard to trust people, turn against your own religion or culture and have identity issues.)
- How might your life be affected? (Your schoolwork might suffer. You might play truant, pretend to be ill, refuse to go to school or leave your home at all through fear. You might be lonely.)
- How would you feel if you were the only person from your race in the area? (Very conspicuous, afraid, alone, with no friends. You might assume everyone from other races is hostile since you've had negative experiences before.)
- If the race you are from is not important, what is important about people? (How they behave towards you, how kind they are, the kind of person they are or become, whether they are doing their best with the resources and talents that they have, to what use they put those talents and how they live their life.)
- Why is it important to stop racism?
- What can *you* do to stop racism?

Challenge

Ask the children to spend a day in school wearing a silly hairstyle or having one sleeve or trouser leg rolled up. How does their peers' and teachers' behaviour change towards them? How would they feel if they were the only one in the school looking like that? (For their safety the children should not go home looking silly – they might be picked on by children from another school.)

Application

8

Assertiveness and self-protection

Personal rights

In 1948 the United Nations drew up a charter called *The Universal Declaration of Human Rights*. These are rights that everyone in the world should have to help prevent suffering in life. There are so many of them they are divided into categories such as the right to security that protects people against crimes; legal rights that protect people from unlawful imprisonment; liberty rights that allow people to speak their minds freely and choose their religion; equality rights that are related to non-discrimination and welfare; or social rights such as the right for children to be educated, the right to food, shelter and warmth. Subsequent treaties include group rights of protection – the protection of ethnic groups against genocide, and the ownership by countries of their national territories and resources.

In 1989 the United Nations adopted *The Convention of the Rights of the Child* stating that children had the right to good food, clean water, a decent place to live, medical attention and to be with their family or whoever else could care for them best. Children should not be used as cheap labour or as child soldiers and should be protected against violence and exploitation; they have a right to speak their own language and practise their own religion and culture.

These rights are related to laws that have been written by, and are upheld by, people in authority. Personal rights (see opposite) can only be upheld by individuals – and by caring people who are with them. By being aware of these rights, and making use of them, children can command respect and gain high self-esteem while preventing other people from controlling them or denying them the right to be themselves. However, children must remember that everyone else has these rights too!

Advice

Children are assertive when they communicate clearly and honestly, handle awkward situations skilfully, are non-judgemental, protect themselves from put–downs and bullying, and respect other people as well as themselves.

Explain about human rights and children's rights.

Activity 1

Ask the children to work in groups of three or four to draw up a list of personal rights they think everyone should have – these are different to the rights already discussed and are to do with the way they are treated by the people around them. Discuss the suggestions and produce a single list of rights that individuals should have.

Personal rights:

- I have the right to say what I need.
- I have the right to say what things are most important to me.
- I have the right to do well without worrying about others being jealous.
- I have the right to say no.
- I have the right to ask for help or to ask for more time to think when I have to make an important decision.
- I have the right to say, 'I don't know' or, 'I don't understand', without others making me feel silly.
- I have the right to make up my own mind about things.
- I have the right to change myself.
- I have the right to make mistakes, as long as they're not done on purpose.
- I have the right to move on from past mistakes without everyone reminding me of them.
- I have the right to be treated with respect.

Activity 2

Ask the children to make posters of these rights to display in school.

Assertiveness

Behaviour can be roughly classed in three groups: aggressive (hostile), passive (timid) and assertive.

Aggressive children think mainly, or only, of themselves and about getting what they want, no matter what the consequences. A form of aggression is passive aggression where the child is manipulative or nasty in a sly, underhand way such as spreading unkind gossip or starting malicious rumours. Aggressive children don't worry about hurting other people's feelings and often blame people or put them down.

Passive children think too much about other people and too little of themselves. They are afraid to say no, to stand up for themselves – and other people – and to go against what the majority do, in case they incur disapproval. They also fear stating their own needs or setting priorities and often hope that someone will guess what they want. Instead of declaring how hurt they feel they will sulk, and instead of asking for something outright they will try to get it in a roundabout way.

Assertive children state how they feel without embarrassment, can express their needs clearly and they respect the other person's right to refuse. Assertive children look for making improvements in their lives rather than blaming others for something going wrong or blaming themselves for not being good enough. They are less prone to self-doubt, low self-esteem, anxiety and depression.

Discuss what it means to be aggressive, passive and assertive. Which behaviour best describes each child in the class/group? (Most people have a mixture of behaviours.)

Discuss the advantages and disadvantages of each of these behaviours. (*See Table opposite*)

Discuss the way people speak. (Aggressive people often start their sentences in an accusing manner, 'You always . . .' and, 'You never . . .' Passive people often over-apologize and show doubt, 'Are you sure?' and, 'Do you really think so?' Assertive people often state how they feel, 'I felt hurt when . . . ')

Advice

	Being aggressive	Being passive	Being assertive
Advantages	It can protect you when you feel threatened or are in danger.	It can be useful to run away when you are threatened with a weapon, or to keep silent when an elderly person upsets you as they are unlikely to change their ways.	It is good to stick up for yourself and for your friends; you earn self-respect and other people's respect. You can put right misunderstandings; you can share how you feel. You are able to behave as though you are confident even when you are not – people will still relate to you as a confident person. You are trusted and people will feel safe confiding in you.
Disadvantages	It can lose you friends and the respect of others; you might say or do something you later regret; you might find relationships are harder to repair and you might find it hard to stay employed or out of trouble.	You can be taken advantage of or bullied. It can lower your self-esteem as your needs are rarely, if ever, met and you are more likely to become depressed.	None – the assertive person knows when it's appropriate to get angry and when it's appropriate to be passive.

Saying no

At times it can be very hard for children to say no. They might feel guilty and awkward about disappointing someone and might believe that they must always say yes for people to like them. They might be desperate to have friends, fearing losing them if they don't comply with their wishes. But, in the long term, agreeing with everything will make children unhappy and they will lose other people's respect.

Before responding to a request, children should consider the following points:

- What it is that they are being asked and what are the consequences of their refusal?

- Who is doing the asking? Is it their dad asking them to help with a five-minute job – something they could easily do? Or is it a close friend who's asking an enormous favour that they will need time to think about before agreeing to do it?

- What is the frequency of the requests? If someone asks a child all the time for help with homework and that person is only interested in the answers, not in understanding how they got those answers, then it is clear the child is being used. By always helping out with work and other things, the child is too available and the other person does not learn to be independent and responsible.

- How do they feel about doing the thing that's asked of them? If they know the request is fair and they don't mind doing it then they could go ahead. But if they feel they are being asked to do something they shouldn't (such as doing something criminal or having sex before they are ready), then they should say no and stick to it.

When saying no, children should look as though they mean it. They should maintain eye contact, sound firm and adopt a confident posture.

Advice

Discuss the following questions with the class:

- Do you usually do things other people around your age ask you to do? If so, why? Do you ever say no?

- Do you have trouble getting other people to accept your refusal? If so, why do you think that is? (You are not firm enough, you've let them persuade you to change your mind before, you feel guilty about saying no, you are afraid of losing friends, your body language does not show that you mean no.)

Activity

Ask the children to sit in pairs and talk about a time when they wanted to say no but were persuaded to change their minds. Then ask them to discuss whether they have ever tried to get someone else to change their mind. Did they do this because they felt it would be good for the other person or to help them in some way?

Role play

Ask for two volunteers, A and B, to role-play how A persuaded B to change his/her mind using one of their scenarios or the suggestion below. Discuss the mistakes B made. For example:

A: 'Can I borrow your maths homework?'

B: 'This is the third time in a row you've asked. I told you last week I won't lend it to you again.'

A: 'Just this time. This is what friends are for.'

B: 'You won't understand the work.'

A: 'You can explain it to me later.'

B (Speaking unhappily): 'OK.'

Repeat the role play showing how B sticks to saying no:

A: 'Can I borrow your maths homework?'

B: 'No.'

A: 'Go on. Let me have it.'

B: 'I mean it. No. Please respect my decision.'

A: 'OK.'

Note: needing to say no does not apply to reasonable requests from teachers and parents!

Application

Feedback and criticism

Feedback is letting children know how they are doing – such as with homework, a school report and in relationships. It tells children what they're doing right, so that they can do more of the same, and what they are doing wrong, so that they can change their ways.

If children are criticized unfairly they must challenge the other person for the sake of their self-esteem and so that resentment doesn't build up, which could ruin the friendship. Also, an unchallenged critic will believe the disparagement is justified and may keep repeating the same comments.

When children criticize they need to be sure of their ground, and be very clear and specific in what they say so that they are not labelling the whole person but a part of their overall behaviour – and they should try to make the criticism constructive. If the other person rejects their criticism with evidence to prove the contrary, they must back down, apologize, and say they'd misunderstood or that they hadn't seen the bigger picture or that they were simply being unfair.

Type of criticism	Action
Justifiable.	Apologize and try to put things right.
Wholly unfair.	Ask the other person for evidence for saying such a thing. Explain why the criticism is unfair and request an apology.
Partly unfair.	Acknowledge any fault and deny what is not true.
Unclear. For example:	Ask for clarification.
'You're selfish.'	'When have I been selfish?'
'You never let me have a go on your Nintendo.'	'Are you talking about yesterday? I wanted to finish part of my game before saving it and then it was time for you to go home. I let you play on it last week. And I said you could play on it first next time.'

Discuss the following questions with the class:

- What is feedback?

- Why is feedback important?

- Give an example of positive feedback (a compliment) and of negative feedback (a criticism).

- What things should you think about when you give negative feedback?

- Saying, 'You're selfish', is an example of unclear criticism. What should you do if someone gives you unclear criticism?

- Think of a time when someone criticized you. How did you feel about it? Was the criticism fair? If it was fair, did you apologize for your behaviour? If it was unfair, did you challenge the person?

- What would happen if you let people criticize you unfairly without you challenging them?

Role play

Ask for two volunteers, A and B. B is often late, forgets pens, pencils and books and keeps borrowing off A, and finds it hard to concentrate. A criticizes B, while B responds appropriately. Give A and B their own scripts and discuss each criticism with the rest of the class as they perform the role play.

Criticism	A	B
Fair	'Why don't you listen more carefully, then you won't have to keep asking me what the teacher said?'	'You're right, I should. I'm sorry.'
Unfair	'Why don't you buy your own pens?'	'I do. I just forget them.'
Partly unfair	'You're always late.'	'I'm not always late. I wasn't late yesterday or Friday.'
	'OK, sorry. You're often late.'	'Yeah.'
Unclear	'I'm fed up with you.	'What do you mean?'
	You're always asking to borrow things.'	'You're right. I'm sorry. I'll try harder to remember my own stuff.'

Invite other volunteers to role-play scenarios from their own life showing how they handled being criticized and then how they could have dealt with it more skilfully.

What is bullying?

Bullying is aggressive behaviour that involves repeatedly physically or emotionally hurting someone else or making them feel uncomfortable. There is usually an imbalance of power where one child, or group of children, oppresses another child or group of children. The bully might find the act amusing or pleasurable while the victim experiences fear and humiliation. Occasionally a child provokes another child into bullying them through a lack of awareness of what is appropriate behaviour.

Bullies experience a need to dominate other children and are often defiant, disaffected with school, dislike rules, have a problem with handling anger or jealousy, might behave impulsively and might have low empathy for others (see page 76). Some bullies – particularly children who bully verbally – are thought highly of by adults as the bullying behaviour is hidden. These children are often considered popular by their peers; indeed, part of their success at bullying can be because they are so popular and witnesses are too afraid of losing the bully's favour to intervene.

Children who have experienced problems at home such as abuse, unemployment, divorce, imprisonment, violence, alcoholism and bereavement, or who have not had effective parenting or good parenting role models are more likely to bully than children from stable and happy home backgrounds. Sometimes over-privileged children bully because they do not see the worth in other people and think too much of their own importance. When children get involved in gangs they might carry out aggressive behaviour to curry favour with the gang members and to feel included. Sometimes children bully because they are impulsive and lack control and fail to consider the consequences before they act. Victims sometimes become bullies themselves, repeating behaviour that was carried out on them.

Advice

Discuss the following questions with the class:

- What is bullying?

- In what ways do people bully? (Physical bullying such as tripping up, pushing, punching and kicking, damaging possessions or throwing them out of a window, forcing someone to do a 'dare', extortion, making comments involving prejudices and name-calling, splitting up of friendships, spreading rumours, gossiping and shunning people, sexual harassment and cyber bullying – using mobile phones and the internet to victimize someone.)

- Why do some children bully?

- Why are some children victims? (Children can be picked on by chance. Very often shy, timid children, with few or no friends to support them, are singled out as they make easy targets. Children who are not sporty or well coordinated are often ridiculed, as are high achievers.)

- How might someone feel if they are being bullied? (Scared, lonely, sad, worthless, stupid, weak.)

- Sometimes bullies excuse their behaviour by saying it was only a bit of fun. Is this really true? (If the child at the receiving end of the 'fun' does not find it fun and is made to feel scared or hurt or upset then it's bullying.)

- Have you witnessed bullying? What did you do? (You should stand up for the victim and encourage others to join you. Get adult help.)

- What could you do if you are the friend of a bully? (Don't go along with the bullying; try to find out what's behind it. Suggest other ways of coping with emotional pain such as talking about feelings, getting angry with a pillow instead of a person, getting help from an adult who will listen.)

- What could you do to protect potential victims? (Don't leave them on their own. Invite them to join you.)

Application

Protecting children from being bullied

Victims should not verbally or physically attack a bully as this can increase a bully's aggression. They should tell an adult about all physical bullying and about any verbal bullying that can't be resolved quickly. They could surround themselves with supportive friends – over 70 per cent of bullying stops when children try to stop the bullying because the bully sees them as not supporting their actions.

When responding to verbal bullying, victims should avoid starting sentences with: 'You . . .' as this is aggressive. So instead of saying: 'You'll pay for this', victims could say: 'I won't forget this.' And instead of labelling the bully by saying: 'You're a thug', victims could say, 'I don't appreciate thuggish behaviour.' Young children might find it helpful to say: 'I don't like it when you're mean', rather than: 'You're mean.' It is not helpful to treat one kind of negative behaviour with another kind.

Victims can shrink a verbal bully's power by agreeing with the bully: 'Yes. I am fat', deliberately misunderstanding the bully: 'That's so kind of you to say that', and making a joke: 'You said you'd rearrange my face for me. How much do you charge? Have you recommendations from satisfied clients?' They can also deflect insults: 'You know, it's OK to be different', ask questions: 'Does saying that make you feel good?', make the bully feel uncomfortable: 'Did someone have a go at you before you got to school this morning?', talk about feelings: 'I feel hurt when you say things like that. Do you mean to hurt me?', and be sympathetic towards the bully: 'You must be hurting inside to say that to me. Do you want to talk about it?' Victims can also be direct: 'Stop being unkind to me.'

Discuss the following questions with the class:

- What kinds of things have bullies done to you? How did you respond? Was the way you handled it successful?

- Have you ever intervened in a bullying situation by telling the bully that they are being nasty or by protecting someone from further attack or by running to get adult help? If so, what happened? If not, why not?

- Would you help protect anyone from being bullied or just a close friend?

- How have you felt when friends have not stuck up for you?

- Research has shown that if, when bullying starts, bystanders try to help and support the victim most bullying stops. Staying quiet, or even walking away from the situation, makes the bullies think you are really supporting them. Laughing with them further encourages them. Knowing this, would you now make more effort to help a victim?

- If you are friends with someone who bullies, have you ever tried to stop them from hurting someone else? Have you ever tried to talk about why they feel the need to bully? Bullies need help, like victims do, but for different reasons.

- Have you ever made sexist, racist or homophobic comments? (Sexism is treating girls/boys as though they have certain negative attributes solely because they are girls/boys. Racism is treating people from another race as though they are inferior and ascribing negative traits that have somehow become stereotyped. Homophobia is treating any non-heterosexual as inferior and making judgements about how they live and how they behave. See also page 90.)

Activity

Invite the children to suggest verbal comments that might be used in bullying. Write these on the board. In small groups, ask the children to make up assertive responses to these comments.

Application

Social safety

Children can't be supervised all the time and increasingly need independence. To keep them safe they need clear rules to follow, and they need to understand the purpose of those rules.

Through the internet, paedophiles can be brought into children's homes and bedrooms via a web cam. By posting photos of themselves, boys and girls can attract the attention of paedophiles posing as young people who inveigle their way on to friends' lists to infiltrate the group and then hone in on one child in particular. Initially, 'conversations' are on neutral subjects that gain the child's trust. Then paedophiles ask more personal questions related to sexual activity. Some might persuade children to undress in front of the web cam in return for expensive 'presents' bought on their behalf online.

It is safer for children to 'chat' in a busy room in the home rather than in the privacy of their bedroom, especially if using a web cam, then paedophiles will see that adults are around. Children should not add anyone to their friends' list whom they haven't personally met, should always use a non-gender specific pseudonym – so they shouldn't post photos of themselves anywhere on the internet – and should never give any information about where they are based or are going in the real world. Paedophiles obtaining details of a day out could stalk the town until they recognize the child from the internet. Any mention of what school they go to can bring a paedophile to the school gates at the end of the day. Children should also be extremely wary of agreeing to actually meet people they have met in the virtual world. Anything worrying should be reported to the police.

Discuss the following questions with the class:

- What safety rules have you been given by your parents? (Suggestions: Never go anywhere without permission, know, or carry on me, my parents' contact telephone numbers and always tell my parents where I am going and with whom. Wear a watch and if an arrangement is changed, I must let my parents know; don't talk to strangers or let them know my name or where I live. If someone has upset me or made me feel uneasy, I should tell my parents – I must make them listen by explaining it's important and not let myself be put off.) Why do these rules exist?

- You get home from school to find no one at home and you don't have your own door key. What would you do? (Ask yourself: Where might Mum or Dad be? Can I contact them by phone? Is there somewhere I can go to wait until they come home? If you go to a friend's or neighbour's house to wait, put a note through your door saying where you've gone. Don't go into anyone's home if you don't feel comfortable with that person, even if it's pouring with rain. If walking to your friend's house, walk confidently.)

- Do you know how to use a public pay phone? (No one should totally rely on mobile phones.) If you don't, ask someone to show you!

- You have met someone on the internet and he asks to meet you. Where would you arrange to meet? (Nowhere unless you have your parents' permission. Then meet the new person with them.)

- What are the dangers of chatting over the internet?

Activity

Make posters showing general safety rules and internet safety rules.

9

Motivation

Personal motivation

When in school, children are rewarded for positive behaviour and for achieving and are usually punished through criticism for bad behaviour and for underachieving. The teacher is in charge of their time in the class and children are motivated through praise and the desire to receive a good report, do well in class tests and end-of-year examinations and gain qualifications.

At home, parents often cajole children into spending time in a positive way by saying, 'When you've done this, we can . . . ' This provides a goal and a reward once that goal has been achieved. But what happens when children are left to make their own choices? Do they carry on doing something that involves achievement and then reward themselves afterwards, or do they slouch on the sofa and watch TV or play electronic games? Very often, children are unable to motivate themselves to do something taxing, always preferring the route of least effort.

For children to feel motivated there has to be a goal – otherwise, what's the point? And the goal has to be something that they care about. Challenge the children to find ways of motivating themselves to do things they are not keen on doing but will benefit them in some way. How can they make themselves care about them more? And what could they ask their teachers and parents to do or say that would help them?

Advice

*Although children can be bribed to work or to achieve,
in the long term they need to recognize personal incentives –
which are usually reaching the end of goals and enjoying the
rewards that go with achieving those goals.*

Discuss the following questions with the class:

- How do you spend your weekends? How much time do you spend
  on homework, exercise, hobbies, interests, socializing and playing?
  (The older you get, the more time you should spend on homework.
  The other things should be in abundance, keeping you busy, involved
  and stimulated.)

- Do you feel that you have the right balance in your life? Are you doing
  the right amount of school work, taking the right amount of exercise,
  spending the right amount of time with friends and spending the right
  amount of time playing with other people and by yourself? How will
  you know that you are? (You will be reaching, or nearly reaching, your
  personal potential in school. You will divide your free time between
  plenty of other activities and have friends you see regularly. You will
  feel happy or contented much of the time.)

- What do you think the consequences are of not having the right
  balance in your life? (If you are doing too much work at the expense of
  exercise and socializing, you will be unfit and feel unhappy and lonely.
  If you are doing too little work and too much of the other things, you
  will underachieve and might get into trouble in school and at home –
  and you might believe you are no good at school work so have low
  expectations of what you could do with your life.)

- What are goals? (Objectives: things to aim for or to focus on. For example,
  to improve your skills, your ability, your knowledge or your lot in life.)
  Why do people have them? (To give them purpose, something to aim for
  and to gain the reward of reaching that goal.)

Application

Increasing motivation

Some children believe that great fortune will befall them and that this good luck will change their life for ever, solve all their problems and make them happy. But even if they do happen to win the lottery or an exotic holiday at some time in the future, it does not mean that they will be any happier.

If things in life come very easily they are often not appreciated; they can be taken for granted. But when children have had to strive to achieve a particular goal, they value that goal so much more and it raises their self-esteem as they can feel very proud of themselves for achieving it.

Often, if children have sufficient determination, they can overcome enormous barriers to achieving a particular goal despite the fact that many people have predicted they will never make it. Unlike children who give in as soon as it starts to get tough – or withdraw from the sight of the goal without even attempting to try for it – these children know that they have the power within themselves to make changes and to improve and they focus with great intensity on what reaching that goal would mean for them.

Reasons why some children fail to achieve their goals include feeling half-hearted about the goal, the goal is unrealistic, they give up very easily, they have low self-esteem and limit their own potential by doubting their ability, they have problems with anxiety or depression which prevent them from striving, they make excuses to themselves as to why they can't reach that goal, they are limited by poor health or a disability or they believe unkind things other people have said about their abilities and don't try to prove them wrong.

Discuss the following questions with the class:

- Do you dream of winning the lottery? Why? In what way would it change your life? Is it realistic to believe that, one day, you will win a great deal of money?

- Do you hope for some huge piece of luck to shape your future or do you believe that what your future becomes is largely up to you?

- What personal qualities are needed to reach goals? (Drive or energy; motivation and determination; self-confidence, self esteem and self-belief; adaptability – if a setback happens you might need to change to overcome it; persistence – you keep trying; staying focused – you don't get distracted into doing something else instead; courage – keeping going in the face of adversity.)

- What purpose do life challenges serve? (They can make people miserable if some tragedy befalls them, although some people have shown great fortitude as a result and have become stronger. Less traumatic challenges give people something to strive towards and a purpose in their personal life. Any challenge, when met, can make people stronger and more confident. People who avoid challenges have no opportunity to grow or to get to know themselves better and how they react when under pressure.)

- Is there anything that you can do to help achieve your goals? (Imagine yourself reaching that longed-for goal and imagine life with that goal achieved. Think positively and believe that you can, in time, reach that goal through your own efforts and persistence. Push doubts aside. Choose realistic goals that are achievable for you so that you don't lose confidence through failure.)

Application

Setting goals

Once children have a goal in mind, they should check whether it is a realistic goal for them – one that is achievable with their personal resources and abilities. They should think about the things they will need to do to reach that goal and put these steps in sequence. Breaking up goals into steps helps to guide children to that goal and gives them a sense of satisfaction once they reach each step, motivating them to carry on.

Sometimes the steps to a particular goal don't work out – either children have trouble reaching a particular step or they no longer want the goal they previously had in mind. They can make an adjustment for what's achievable for them or adapt the goal to suit their change of need.

If children have a long-term goal – one that will take them several years to reach – they should break it up into smaller goals, each with their individual steps. This helps to keep children on target and gives them rewards at regular intervals to keep them motivated.

If children feel very determined about reaching a goal, they should try not to let other people put them off. However, this does not mean that children shouldn't listen to advice on whether something is realistic for them. They could test the theory, if they like, to see how they do on the first step of their goal. They can always change direction if it really won't work out for them.

Goals children frequently make are related to helping them get good qualifications that will take them on to further education or to training after leaving school, making and keeping friends, getting a boyfriend/girlfriend, and saving for a school trip or a new toy or gadget.

Advice

Activity

As a class or in small groups, ask the children to write a goal plan for someone who either wants to cook a meal for the first time or wants to learn to drive. Suggestions:

Cooking a meal	Learning to drive
Read recipe books to find something that is easy to do and people at home would like to eat.	Get a job and save money for your lessons (unless you have someone to pay for them for you).
Find an adult to help you.	Ask at home if an experienced driver will give you practice on a car outside the lessons, to help you.
Get permission to try that recipe.	Apply for and obtain your provisional driving licence.
Agree on a time when you can cook.	Get a copy of *The Highway Code* and start learning the information inside the book.
Write a shopping list.	Find out the prices of lessons with different companies or individuals.
Buy the items on the list.	Ring up to make arrangements for your first lesson.
Get out the equipment that you will need.	Have more lessons and practise in between.
Read the recipe through so that you know the order to do things in and understand what kind of things you will need to do.	Pass the theory examination.
Prepare all the food. Sometimes you can prepare some and while that's cooking you can carry on preparing the rest of the food.	In consultation with your driving instructor, enter for your test.
Keep checking the recipe to make sure that you are doing everything right.	Practise even more.
When you have finished, tidy up the kitchen.	Sit your driving test.
Enjoy the meal with your family.	Celebrate passing. Be sure to drive very carefully because now you are on your own!

Application

10 Managing anxiety and depression

Managing anxiety and panic

Children need help if their anxiety is bad enough to affect their ability to live a normal life. Children with autism spectrum disorders are more prone to anxiety and they should not be forced to do something they feel anxious about.

Anxiety is related to the 'fight or flight' mechanism which allows people to perform well in a crisis – and in competitive sports and examinations – by producing adrenaline. However, if children suffer from anxiety, too much adrenaline is produced making them feel ill and creating a spiral of increasing anxiety as they wory over their symptoms. This causes more adrenaline to be released which causes more anxiety, which in turn causes more adrenaline to be released. If this circle of anxiety is unbroken it can lead to a panic attack.

A panic attack is an extreme response to an anxious event, and it can turn into a phobia. Symptoms of a panic attack include abdominal and chest pain, feeling nauseous and being sick, feeling very hot or cold, feeling dizzy or faint, needing frequent visits to the toilet, a rapid heart beat, shaking, sweating and quick, shallow breathing, known as hyperventilation.

Stopping hyperventilation – the taking in of too much oxygen and the breathing out of too much carbon dioxide – by either breathing into a paper bag or using diaphragmatic breathing helps to restore the body's natural balance of gases in the blood and so eases symptoms of anxiety. Mouth breathing leads to hyperventilation – although is unavoidable when people talk – so it is important for children to breathe in through their nose. Hyperventilation can exacerbate the symptoms of asthma sufferers.

Advice

Stress, anxiety and depression are very common difficulties so it is useful for children to learn coping strategies, for now and for future challenges.

Teach the children how to breathe diaphragmatically using the instructions below as a guide. It is essential you learn this technique and are adept at using it before you teach it.

Are you hyperventilating?

- Put one hand on your tummy and one hand on your chest. If the hand on your chest moves when you breathe, you are hyperventilating.

- Count the number of breathing cycles you have in a minute – breathing in and then out counts as one cycle. It is normal to have 12 cycles per minute when at rest, such as when sitting in the classroom. If you are breathing more than this, check you are breathing deeply and diaphragmatically and are breathing through your nose – it takes longer than mouth breathing.

Diaphragmatic breathing

Everyday breathing should be done through the nose so that the hairs in the nose can filter out dust and other particles and the air can be warmed and moistened before reaching the lungs.

Slowly breathe in through your nose, with your mouth closed, to a count of four. The hand on your chest should not move and your abdominal muscles should push out the hand on your tummy. Exaggerate the in breath by pushing out your tummy as far as it will go. As you breathe out (through your mouth if you wish), to a count of four, your tummy should fall back to its natural position. The air should not be forced out.

Imagine drawing a circle in your mind where the first half of the circle is for breathing in and the second half for breathing out. It is important not to breathe in before you have finished breathing out. Keep breathing like this as often as you can, for as long as you can.

Application

Managing stress

Stress is anything that causes pressure in children, such as having parents argue or separate, having a parent with a health problem, bereavement, going through puberty, worrying about examinations, changing school, moving house and breaking up with a friend.

Children should be encouraged to talk about their concerns rather than bottling them up – as that will make them internalize their problems which will affect their mental health. They should share their concerns with a sympathetic, understanding and non-judgemental adult. With support, they will find stress easier to cope with.

Children who are perfectionists, very ambitious, impatient, competitive, high achievers, self-critical, hardworking and who dislike changes to routine are more prone to stress and are said to have personality type A. Children who are steady, calm and relaxed and not terribly ambitious are less prone to stress and are said to have personality type B. Children might be a mix of the two personality types, although one will probably predominate. Children who are mainly type A need to be encouraged to take life in a more leisurely and relaxed way and should be steered away from absolute perfectionism.

The way stress affects the body includes sweating, trembling, a rapid heartbeat, frequently needing to go to the toilet, butterflies in the stomach, headaches, back or neck pain, and skin problems, such as eczema, psoriasis or more acne than usual. Stressed children can't learn, so ensure that your lessons do not increase children's stress.

Discuss the following questions with the class:

- What is stress? What kinds of things cause stress?

- Are some people more prone to stress than others?

- How does stress affect the body?

Activity

Techniques people use to manage stress are grouped together and called 'coping mechanisms'. Help the children to make a list of their coping mechanisms. Suggestions to include:

Coping mechanisms	Description
Changing thoughts.	People prone to stress often have very negative thoughts which increase their stress. Instead they should think, 'I'm nervous about doing this but I will feel very proud of myself afterwards for trying my hardest.'
Prioritizing worries.	Write a list of all your worries and put them in order. Some things just aren't worth worrying about, so make a conscious effort not to waste time and energy on them. For very big worries go to an adult for help and advice; endlessly worrying without finding solutions will just increase your stress.
Managing regular schoolwork.	Make sure you do your homework regularly so that it doesn't pile up. If you find it getting on top of you, see your teachers and ask for help.
Planning steady revision for examinations.	Write yourself a revision timetable – but ensure that you put in time to exercise and socialize as well to make it balanced and realistic.
Exercising each day.	Exercise helps reduce stress and raises your mood.
Doing relaxation exercises.	Regular relaxation sessions will help you to stay relaxed through the day and will improve your sleep. (See page 118.)
Learning for the future.	Understand when you are at risk from stress from past experience and take measures to reduce it before it overwhelms you.

Learning to relax

It is not thought possible to teach relaxation techniques to children aged seven and under. Teaching relaxation skills to children with autism spectrum disorders can increase their anxiety, so they need to learn to deal with their anxiety in other ways, such as distraction, time out and physical activity.

Practise the entire relaxation session yourself before guiding the children through it.

Prepare the children for the session by explaining they need to recognize the difference in how tense and relaxed muscles feel. When they are anxious they might be so used to tense muscles that they think their muscles are relaxed when they aren't. They will need to tense different muscle groups, hold them for a slow count of three and then relax them and take time to feel the difference. Practise identifying muscle groups with them so that they will know exactly what to do.

When it comes to tensing abdominal muscles, they will need to pull hard on their tummy, tense their pelvic floor muscles – the ones that stop them urinating and defecating – and their buttocks while pushing their lower back into the floor.

Tell the children they will need to breathe diaphragmatically throughout the exercise. Explain how to do this (see page 115) – and keep reminding them of their breathing during the session.

To carry out the relaxation sequence, children should lie on their backs on soft gym mats with their eyes closed, their arms by their sides, their fingers gently curled and their legs slightly apart. In a classroom environment, children could try the exercise sitting with their heads resting on their arms over a desk. Once they have learned what to do in school, they could repeat the exercise at home, lying on their bed.

Here is the order of muscle groups to tense. After asking the children to tense a particular group say, 'Hold to the count of three: one . . . two . . . three. Let go and feel the tension leave your . . . Notice how it feels to have a relaxed . . .'

- Screw up your face . . .
- Tense your neck and shoulders . . .
- Tense one arm and hand . . .
- Tense the other arm and hand . . .
- Tense your chest muscles . . .
- Pull your stomach in hard and pull hard on the muscles that stop you going to the toilet. Clench your bottom muscles while still holding the other muscles tight and push the lower part of your back into the floor . . .
- Tense one leg and foot . . .
- Tense the other leg and foot . . .
- Tense your whole body. Make sure your face is tense, your chest is tense, your arms and hands are tense, your tummy, bottom and back are tense. Make sure your legs and your feet are tense . . .

Now concentrate on relaxing:

- Concentrate on how your body feels. It feels loose, limp, floppy and relaxed. Your body feels heavy and very relaxed.
- Keep thinking about your body to check that each muscle group is relaxed. Before you mentally leave one muscle group to check the next one, tell yourself how floppy the muscles are and how you feel your face, arm, leg and so on melt into the floor. Let all your tension go.
- Stay like this for 20 minutes, until you are told when the time is up.
- Open your eyes. Slowly start getting feeling back into your muscles. Move your arms and your legs. Slowly sit up and look around you. Stretch your body. When you're ready, slowly stand up and notice how good you feel. You're now wide awake.

School phobia

School phobia is an umbrella term for a range of anxiety disorders – and depression – that contribute to a child refusing school. If forced to go to school, the child suffers a panic attack. School phobia is unrelated to truanting. Children with autism spectrum disorders are especially prone to school phobia and respond to strict routine, time alone, time out doing a preferred activity, and using up physical energy by running errands.

Separation anxiety is a fear of being away from parents: children worry about something happening to their parents or to them. Signs of separation anxiety include becoming nervous about being left alone, finding it hard to get to sleep, fearing burglars and monsters under the bed, needing a light on at night, shadowing parents, distress at parting from parents that continues long after parents leave. Separation anxiety can be triggered by stress from starting school for the first time, being absent from school for a long time from ill health or a holiday, having a new baby in the family, bereavement, having troubles at home, or being bullied.

Agoraphobia is a fear about being in places or situations where escape is not possible, or from where escape might be embarrassing, and in situations where help is not immediately available should you suddenly feel panicky. Children might fear going to school by public transport or going shopping or to the cinema.

Social phobia is a fear of being judged and evaluated by others. In school, children will fear being the centre of attention, having to answer questions or read aloud in class, being involved in assemblies, performances, games lessons and sports day, being picked last for teams and having others laughing at their mistakes or ineptitude.

Discuss the following questions with the class:

- It is common for children to feel anxious about going to school. What kinds of things do they worry about?

- What are the physical symptoms of anxiety? (The number and severity of symptoms vary but commonly include stomach aches, headaches, shaking, frequent urination and defecation, and feeling sick.)

- What is a panic attack? What are the physical symptoms of a panic attack? (More intense symptoms of anxiety previously mentioned, plus crying, diarrhoea, feeling faint, hyperventilation, insomnia, vomiting, a rapid heart beat and sweating.)

- Have you ever experienced a panic attack or know of someone who has? (Although the symptoms are extremely unpleasant, they don't actually harm you. People don't die from panic attacks.)

- What do you understand by the term 'school phobia'?

- What causes school phobia? (Stress that you can't deal with. The way it is expressed is through not wanting to go to school – and later, not wanting to go anywhere else either. Home is viewed as a safe place to be.)

- How could you help someone who has trouble going to school? (Be kind, protect them from being bullied, offer to meet them at school in the mornings or even travel to school with them, look after them when you get to school and try to distract them from their fears, be there for them – don't leave them on their own, show you care by asking them if they are OK and by asking how else you can help. Reassure them, be sympathetic and patient and don't make fun of them or allow others to. Be with them at breaktimes and lunchtimes and include them in games and with your other friends. Arrange to see them out of school too.)

Application

Insomnia

Insomnia is the inability to get to sleep for hours, to stay asleep or to have refreshing sleep. This leaves children feeling unrefreshed and jaded. If they are seriously affected by insomnia, they might not sleep at all during the night. Problems caused by lack of sleep include fatigue, difficulty concentrating and irritability.

Insomnia is most commonly caused by emotional, lifestyle and psychiatric problems, including anxiety, stress, suppressed anger, depression (usually causing early wakening), excitement, having too much caffeine in drinks, keeping erratic hours and losing the body's routine, needing to go to the toilet from drinking late at night, lack of exercise, and psychotic illness, such as being in a manic or depressive state.

It is important for children to accept it if sleep evades them – lack of sleep won't harm them in the short term. In the long term it can cause psychotic symptoms and will need to be treated by a doctor. Children should concentrate on resting and keeping their body relaxed. They can do this by mentally scanning their muscles for tenseness. When they find tense muscles, they should consciously relax them by imagining them as loose, limp and floppy and every time they let out a breath they should imagine their limbs sinking further and further into the bed. They could perform a relaxation routine (such as the one described on page 119).

Discuss the following questions with the class:

- Have you had trouble sleeping? How did that make you feel?
- What kinds of things prevented you from having a good night's sleep?
- What do you think you could do to help you get to sleep, and stay asleep?

Try compiling with the children a list of dos and don'ts to help with insomnia.

Do	Don't
Have a special bedtime routine – a hot bath, a hot drink, a bedtime story or reading something that's not too stimulating.	Watch the clock! It will only make you more anxious about getting to sleep.
Follow a relaxation routine (see page 119).	Take your worries to bed. If you fear you might forget something important for the following day or there's something pressing that needs to be decided upon, write it down and then forget about it – it will still be there in the morning.
Keep your room dark with blackout linings on your curtains or blinds.	Have stimulating conversations before bed.
Keep your room well ventilated and not too warm or too cold.	Exercise in the evening as it can be stimulating, but ensure that you have plenty of exercise through the day.
Ask other household members not to make noise.	Have too much to drink in the evenings so that you avoid having to get up repeatedly to go to the toilet.
Distract your mind by counting back from 100 very slowly. Or count backwards in twos, then threes and so on. Or count down each time you diaphragmatically breathe in (noting how your abdomen rises and your chest remains still).	Have a nap in the daytime to make up for lost sleep – it can put your body clock further out.

Managing depression

Depression is a continued low mood state involving loss of interest and enjoyment that can't be 'snapped out of'. It can follow bereavement, parental divorce or another stressful life event. Sometimes it is triggered by certain illnesses, hormonal disorders/imbalances (such as those caused by birth control pills), tension or stress, chemical imbalances in the brain, thyroid disorders, poor diet and lack of exercise, and by premenstrual and postnatal effects. Sometimes there is no apparent reason for it. Long-term anxiety makes children prone to depression and significantly increases the risks of suicide.

Depression affects social functioning. Children might be unable to express themselves effectively and smile or talk naturally. They might have trouble concentrating and remembering things. They can feel isolated and alone, thinking that no one understands them, and they can feel detached from other people, unable to experience feelings of care others have for them. They can feel sad, hopeless, worthless and useless and might think about death and suicide. They might have bursts of anger or impatience and feel anxious, tired and lethargic.

They might sleep and eat more or less than usual, be unable to motivate themselves, not care about washing and keeping clean, lose interest in things they were previously interested in, be tearful, overwork to dull their mind and have a multitude of physical symptoms such as backaches and headaches.

Some children harm themselves by cutting, carving, burning, branding, scratching and head banging as a way to cope with overwhelming emotions and to transform their emotional distress into physical pain. Although they might feel guilty and ashamed about harming themselves, they cannot help it.

Children experiencing such difficulties should see a doctor as a matter of urgency.

Discuss the following questions with the class:

- What is depression? What causes it?

- Are some people more prone to depression than others?

- How does depression affect the way someone behaves?

- How does depression affect someone's thoughts?

- What is the main risk of untreated depression? (Suicide.)

- Do you know someone who has depression? How does it affect them?

- What can be done about depression?

With the children's help, compile a list of things they can do to help guard themselves against becoming depressed.

Things to help guard against depression	Details
Try to see your problems objectively.	Consider how other people would see you and your life – is it the bleak picture you are giving yourself?
Avoid labelling yourself negatively.	Are you as useless or as worthless as you believe? Look for evidence to disprove it rather than to prove it. See mistakes as learning experiences.
Be optimistic.	Believe that an unhappy past does not mean you will have an unhappy future. Things will get better.
Don't spend all day in bed.	Lack of exercise contributes to depression and being in bed does not allow you to achieve anything which will make you feel better.
Eat sensibly.	Don't overeat, under-eat or go for long periods without food.
Have a routine.	Give your day purpose and keep it balanced. Do schoolwork, see friends, take exercise, enjoy a hobby and have some time to yourself to achieve balance in your life.
Have interests.	Make sure you do something you enjoy every day.
Keep up with friends.	Social isolation invites depression. Avoid people who are unkind and seek out people who are good to be with. Tell them how you feel.
Don't take on too much.	Be extra kind to and patient with yourself. Don't set yourself up for failure by overwhelming yourself with work.

Resilience

To be resilient, children must feel secure, have inner strength and believe in their own abilities (and have good communication skills).

Children feel secure because they know they are loved and that family and non-family members, such as teachers and doctors, can support them in times of need and can look after their best interests. Their parents have shown them how they should behave, lead their lives and deal with other people, encouraging them to be independent while understanding times when they are scared and want reassurance. Their parents set clear boundaries so that the children know what they should and should not do and their home lives have structure and routine.

Children have inner strength because they know that they are lovable with qualities that others value and that they have the power to make a difference in their lives and in other people's lives. They care about and feel proud of themselves. They know what to do or where to go for help to solve problems. They know they are responsible for the things they do and are prepared to take the consequences of their actions should they be wrong. They believe in themselves and the power within them to take care of themselves; they see their future in a positive light.

Children have confidence in their personal abilities because they interact well with other people and can express themselves and understand other people well. They are socially confident and can identify the right person to help with their problems if they can't solve them alone. They are aware of how they feel about things and where their limitations lie. They can manage their behaviour so that it does not become destructive and they can stop impulsive behaviour they might later regret.

Advice

Discuss the following questions with the class:

- What is resilience? (Someone is said to be resilient when they have the ability to recover from stress and catastrophe and to cope with adversity. People who aren't resilient can feel fearful, lonely and vulnerable.)

- How do resilient people think and behave? (They regard mistakes as learning experiences, see difficulties in life as challenges to be overcome rather than scary things to be avoided, and they believe they have the ability and strength to overcome them, being aware of their personal strengths. For things outside their control, they accept what can't be changed. They can set realistic goals and have realistic expectations of what they can achieve. They are empathetic and respect and care about other people, and other people respect and care about them. They have good social skills, can share their feelings and are not afraid to compliment other people. They are happy with themselves and believe they are lovable.)

- How well do you cope when you are challenged by life – or when something goes wrong? Do you 'bounce back' easily?

- What things have challenged you in your life? What happened to you as a result?

- How can you increase your resilience? (Exercise regularly, try new things, join clubs and spend time with friends, work hard at your relationships, be ready with compliments, be respectful and expect respect back, learn from past mistakes, be kind to yourself and others, try to put right mistakes, don't be afraid to say sorry to patch up relationships, share feelings, seek help from other people, have plenty of interests, do things that make you proud of yourself, set realistic goals, look for solutions to problems, don't give up, be positive.)

Application

Coping with change

Separation and divorce

Today, one in two marriages end in divorce. Children whose own parents divorced are more likely to divorce themselves. Because divorce is no longer a social taboo people opt for this more quickly rather than try to work things out and fewer people than in previous generations are now prepared to stay in an unhappy marriage.

When couples with children split up there is less money for the custodial parent to live on so the family home might have to be sold to provide two households and the children might have to move area and change schools. Some children might have to be taken into care or be brought up by a relative if neither parent can house them or care for them. Relationships children had with extended family members can change for the worse, and with the removal of a partner from the family home there is also the possibility of a loss of a role model, parenting skills, general skills and support from the extended family of that parent.

Children from divorced families are less likely to do well in school, have poorer mental health, lower self-esteem and more problems with their relationships than children from intact families. Pre-teenagers might get involved in drug or alcohol misuse and truanting, while teenagers might become sexually active earlier and be involved in delinquent behaviour. However, not all children affected by divorce have these problems – and some children have them regardless of their parents divorcing.

Children of separating and divorcing parents may feel betrayed, hurt, angry, sad, rejected, abandoned, fearful, confused and they may have little self-worth, feeling unlovable and to blame for what has happened. Sometimes children become withdrawn, depressed and anxious.

Advice

Change can make children feel vulnerable and scared and tests their resilience. However, being able to cope with major changes in childhood gives children valuable experience for adulthood.

Discuss the following questions with the class:

- Have you experienced your parents separating or divorcing? How did you feel about it?

- How could you help friends whose parents are going through separation or divorce? (Talk to them about their feelings. Be understanding if they are grumpy or moody – make allowances. Try to empathize with them and imagine how it would feel if your parents were splitting up or how it felt when they did.)

- What problems might children face when becoming part of a new family or when their family gets 'blended' with another? (Children from each family might be treated differently and there might be step-sibling rivalry, with step-parents not liking the children or the children not taking to them. Children from the two families might have to share rooms, have less time alone with their parent than they used to and have to eat food they might not like, prepared by a step-parent. There might be new rules and they might be told off by someone new. They might still hope that their own parents will get together again.)

- Have you experienced positive outcomes of a newly formed family? (You might benefit from a larger support network of relations as you have step-grandparents and aunts and uncles too now; you might be relieved that the conflict you experienced at home has stopped; you might have escaped from an abusive parent.)

- How could you help a friend whose divorced parent is remarrying? (Talk to them about their feelings. Be understanding if they are grumpy or moody – make allowances. Try to empathize and imagine how you would feel if your mum or dad remarried – or how it felt when they did.)

Application

Bereavement

There are five stages of grief, the first four of which can be experienced in any order:

- Shock/numbness/denial/disbelief.

- Fear and anger – about being left alone to cope and because the life could not be saved.

- Bargaining – with a higher deity: 'If I do . . . let me get over this.'

- Depression – if it's severe there could be a risk of suicide.

- Acceptance.

A child who is not coping with bereavement can get stuck at any of the first four stages, needing help in reaching acceptance of the loss.

Bereaved children can feel guilty if they survived but, for example, their younger sibling did not. Parents can idolize a dead child, making it harder for siblings to believe that their parents love them just as much as they do their dead sibling. Children's identity can be affected if they were a twin or higher multiple, as now their sibling is gone people see them as a single child or a twin instead of a triplet, for example. Losing a grandparent or other relative can be keenly felt if that person played a large role in the child's life.

Losing a baby in the family is very sad so soon after there was so much joy – and the toys are a painful reminder of what has happened. Losing a pet can also be very hard for children, especially if it had always been in their life; the bond can be very strong. It can be very painful for children to lose a friend – especially if the relationship was close. Any violent death or suicide is extremely hard for children to come to terms with – and there is a risk of a copycat suicide.

Discuss the following questions with the class:

- What problems might arise when a child loses a parent? (It redefines the family. The remaining parent – if there is one – might be temporarily lost to the child in his or her own grief. The family might have to move to a smaller house and the remaining parent might have to find work or find a job that fits into family life. There might be more arguments as everyone in the family is struggling to cope. Everyone will have new roles to try to keep the family functioning; all the children will have to grow up more quickly than their peers.)

- What feelings do you think bereaved people might have? (Anger, anxiety, despair, grief, guilt, isolation, loneliness, pining, sorrow, vulnerability and yearning.)

- What could you do to help friends who suffer bereavement? (Stay with them as long as you can, say how sorry you are, ask about what happened, give them a hug, let them cry, say you'll be there for them and visit them regularly, seek them out at school, don't worry if there are silences, try to keep things normal by doing the same kinds of things you used to do together.)

- What are the danger signs that someone is not coping with their loss? (A downward turn in school performance, worries about school, changed behaviour – aggression, anxiety and panic attacks, nightmares, insomnia, transient mutism. Avoidance of talking about the deceased, becoming accident prone for attention or as self-punishment, displaying anti-social behaviour, being socially and emotionally withdrawn, showing signs of depression, feeling unwell with no obvious cause and being unable to function on a day-to-day basis.)

Application

Making difficult decisions

Frequently in life children come to a junction where there could be good arguments for taking either fork. However, they could experience regret if their decision is based on a whim. For example, they might feel hurt and angry over what someone's said and want to end a friendship – yet there might be many good things in the relationship worth saving.

To approach a decision logically, children should set out the pros and cons of making a particular choice and consider how these would affect them or how important the issue is to them. They could give each entry a weighting out of three, where three is reserved for an issue they feel very strongly about, two is used for an important issue and one represents a minor issue.

Then they could add the scores to give two totals. If one decision yields a much larger total than the other, the children should go with that decision. If there is only a difference of one or two points, they should check the weighting or keep things as they are until something happens to adjust the weighting in a dramatic way – to get a clear message about which decision is better to go for.

Advice

Activity

Ask the children to consider, in small groups, whether schools should ban swearing, listing reasons for and against and assigning scores out of three. Young children could just consider how many entries each side has.
Have a vote at the end of the lesson and discuss reasons and weightings.

Against a swearing ban	Score	For a swearing ban	Score
It's too much effort to change things.	3	It could be considered a challenge	1
Swearing reflects today's society – we should accept our changing language.	2	Stopping swearing can reduce other aggressive behaviour.	3
It's no big deal. Everyone does it.	1	Swearing scares and offends people.	3
How could it be policed? It's too big a job.	3	Children would be encouraged to be more imaginative with their choice of words.	2
People have a right to voice their opinions using words of their choice.	2	Feelings can be better expressed using a larger pool of vocabulary.	2
Swearing is only words – it can't really hurt anyone.	1	By stopping swearing, a message of respect is given to all.	3
Swearing shows other people you're upset – it's a useful way of communicating.	2	Getting out of the habit of swearing makes it less likely that children will swear in places where it matters more such as in a place of worship.	3
There are already too many rules in school. Having another would be overkill.	3	An anti-swearing message might be taken home and families might reassess how they operate.	3
		Young children are less likely to pick up swearing if they don't hear it from older children.	3
Total:	**17**	**Total:**	**23**

Carrying decisions through

Once children have made a decision, doubts can still nag at them, especially if they weren't entirely comfortable with that decision. So, it can be helpful for children to have written evidence to remind them why they made that decision in the first place.

For example, one girl might choose to go on a short residential course or on a school trip involving a stay away from home, yet as the time approaches more and more fears crop up, making her want to back out of the venture. If by reminding herself of all the reasons why it is good for her to go, and with the support of adults and kindly friends, that child manages to overcome homesickness or her fears about going on a school trip, she will become emotionally stronger and will worry less about leaving home for good and living independently of her parents at some time in the future.

A teenage boy might decide the best thing to do is to split up with his girlfriend. However, once the deed is done he might change his focus from the reasons why he wanted the break to how lonely he now feels without her. He might decide to make up with her, rather than fill in the lonely times with activities of his own and with seeing friends he might have had too little time for while going out with his girlfriend. The reasons for the split will still be there and by referring to them he can prevent himself from being caught in an unhelpful circle where he has to break up with his girlfriend a second or even a third time.

Advice

Discuss the following questions with the class:

- If you have trouble sticking with a decision, what do you think you could do to help you stay with it longer? (Write down the reasons for your decision to remind you why you made it. Discuss your fears and reservations with family and friends – and anyone else who might be involved. This helps you check your perspective and will give you emotional and practical support through your decision.)

- Have you ever had a friend who had trouble sticking with a decision? If so, what did you do to help? (Remind the friend why they made the decision and what they will get out of the process once the goal has been reached. Reassure them that anyone would find it hard and say how well they are doing. Show them that you believe they can do it. Say that you think they'll regret it if they change their mind when there were sound reasons for making the decision.)

- When people are unsure of whether they have made the right decision, or are having trouble coping, why is it important to step in and help? (People are very vulnerable when they are struggling with something. They might make a decision based on what's easiest rather than what would be best for them.)

Primary to secondary school transfer

Children making the transition from primary to secondary school can feel bewildered. Below are some differences children are likely to find.

Secondary schools are much larger, having more than one building on more than one level and they could be on a 'split site'; some have over 100 teachers, many of whom are male, and over 2,000 pupils. Children will have to learn the routes from each class to the next. They will be split into form groups where registration takes place, although often morning registration is taken by subject teachers, and they will have the same form teacher for a year or more. Not all lessons will be taught in form groupings – mathematics and English are often banded. They will have many new subjects to learn.

Children pay at the canteen, buy vouchers or get smart cards from the school office and it is up to them what they choose to eat at lunchtime – there are no dinner helpers.

Assembly can be in the morning or in the afternoon; the hall might not be large enough to accommodate all pupils so different year groups will have assemblies on different days. Instead of being at the top of the school the children will now be at the bottom; some older children will be prefects. There will be new school rules and strict expectations of conduct on stairs and in corridors.

There will be regular testing in school in most of their subjects and they will have a homework diary to record the work they need to do. Instead of trays or pegs they might be provided with lockers. Children might witness much more undesirable behaviour than they did in primary school. There might be lunchtime and after-school clubs to join, and a homework club.

Advice

Discuss the following questions with the class:

- How do you feel about going to secondary school? (It is normal to feel scared and excited. School will feel strange for a while – in time you will feel a greater sense of belonging. Be wary of 'horror' stories other children tell about the school; they might be exaggerated or wholly untrue.)

- What do you think will be different from primary school? What things will be the same? (Bells ringing to signal ends of lessons, going outside at breaktimes, staff being on duty at breaktimes, reports being sent home, parents' evenings, registration in lessons.)

- What can you do to make the transition less stressful? (Get a plan of the building and study the layout, learn the school rules. Visit the school and meet your form teacher; learn the lesson times, lunchtime, and the start of school and home times. Get photographs of the headteacher, school secretary, your new form teacher and, perhaps, the special educational needs coordinator or inclusion manager. Put your name in your new uniform and ensure that you have a large school bag and appropriate equipment. Read the school's anti-bullying policy if you are concerned about being bullied. Practise travelling to the school several times, especially if you are travelling on public transport for the first time.)

- How could you view the transition in a positive light? (Think of it as a new start with new teachers and new subjects. View the move as a challenge and the school as an exciting and stimulating place to be.)

- Can you think of a personal statement that will help you make the most of yourself? (My daughter's school motto was 'Be the best that you can be' – what more can be asked of you?)

Further reading

Csóti, M. (2001), *Contentious Issues: Discussion Stories for Young People.* London: Jessica Kingsley Publishers.

— (2008), *How to Stop Bullying: Positive Steps to Protect Children in Your Care.* London: Right Way, Constable & Robinson Ltd.

— (2000), *People Skills for Young Adults.* London: Jessica Kingsley Publishers.

— (2003), *School Phobia, Panic Attacks and Anxiety in Children.* London: Jessica Kingsley Publishers.

— (2001), *Social Awareness Skills for Children.* London: Jessica Kingsley Publishers.

Dowling, M. (2005), *Young Children's Personal, Social and Emotional Development.* Second Edition. London: Paul Chapman Publishing.

Goleman, D. (1996), *Emotional Intelligence: Why it can matter more than IQ.* London: Bloomsbury.

Huebner, D. (2006), *What to Do When You Worry Too Much: A Kid's Guide to Overcoming Anxiety.* Washington, D. C: Magination Press.

Joseph, J. (2006), *Learning in the Emotional Rooms: How to create classrooms that are uplifting for the spirit.* Australia: Focus Education Australia Pty Ltd.

Morales, R. (2008), *Empowering Your Pupils through Role-Play: Exploring emotions and building resilience.* Abingdon, Oxfordshire: Routledge (First published 2003 by Curriculum Corporation, Australia).

Moyes, R. A. (2001), *Incorporating Social Goals in the Classroom: A Guide for Teachers and Parents of Children with High-Functioning Autism and Asperger Syndrome.* London: Jessica Kingsley Publishers.

Rae, T. and Pedersen, L. (2007), *Developing Emotional Literacy with Teenage Boys.* London: Paul Chapman Publishing.